ENGLISH COMMUNICATION 10

Q: SKILLS FOR SUCCESS

Susan Earle-Carlin

Series Consultants:
Marguerite Ann Snow
Lawrence J. Zwier

Vocabulary Consultant:
Cheryl Boyd Zimmerman

mazdakhan@yahoo.com

OXFORD
UNIVERSITY PRESS

ACKNOWLEDGEMENTS

Author

Susan Earle-Carlin earned a Ph.D. in Reading, Language, and Cognition from Hofstra University. She has taught at SUNY Old Westbury and Rutgers University and now teaches in the Program in Academic English/ESL at the University of California, Irvine. Her interests include addressing the needs of generation 1.5 students at the university and improving the communication skills of international teaching assistants. *Q* is her third ESL textbook.

Series Consultants

Marguerite Ann Snow holds a Ph.D. in Applied Linguistics from UCLA. She is a Professor in the Charter College of Education at California State University, Los Angeles where she teaches in the TESOL M.A. program. She has published in *TESOL Quarterly*, *Applied Linguistics*, and *The Modern Language Journal*. She has been a Fulbright scholar in Hong Kong and Cyprus. In 2006, she received the President's Distinguished Professor award at Cal State LA. In addition to working closely with ESL and mainstream public school teachers in the U.S., she has trained EFL teachers in Algeria, Argentina, Brazil, Egypt, Japan, Morocco, Pakistan, Spain, and Turkey. Her main interests are integrated content and language instruction, English for Academic Purposes, and standards for English teaching and learning.

Lawrence J. Zwier holds an M.A. in TESL from the University of Minnesota. He is currently the Associate Director for Curriculum Development at the English Language Center at Michigan State University in East Lansing. He has taught ESL/EFL in the U.S., Saudi Arabia, Malaysia, Japan, and Singapore. He is a frequent TESOL conference presenter and has published many ESL/EFL books in the areas of test-preparation, vocabulary, and reading, including *Inside Reading 2* for Oxford University Press.

Vocabulary Consultant

Cheryl Boyd Zimmerman is Associate Professor of TESOL at California State University, Fullerton. She specializes in second language vocabulary acquisition, an area in which she is widely published. She teaches graduate courses on second language acquisition, culture, vocabulary, and the fundamentals of TESOL and is a frequent invited speaker on topics related to vocabulary teaching and learning. She is the author of *Word Knowledge: A Vocabulary Teacher's Handbook* and Series Director of *Inside Reading*, both published by Oxford University Press.

WELCOME!

At ILSC Education Group, we take pride in delivering quality educational programs, using a dynamic approach that responds to your interests, as well as new global developments in technology and thinking. In all of our courses, we encourage you to be active participants. We teach fundamental skills in a way that engages you to learn and that inspires creativity and confidence. For more than 20 years, we have been developing and refining our teaching methods, and they have proven successful with thousands of students from all over the world.

Our goal at ILSC is to prepare you for wherever you want to go in the world by helping you achieve internationally relevant career and language skills. You'll be inspired to make learning a lifelong pursuit.

On behalf of our staff and teachers, we welcome you to ILSC. You are about to begin an exciting adventure in learning!

ILSC Global Directors and Academic Team

ilsc LANGUAGE SCHOOLS

SCOPE AND SEQUENCE | English Communication 10

UNIT	LISTENING	SPEAKING	VOCABULARY
1 Change **Q How do people react to change?** **LISTENING 1: The Reindeer People** A Radio Documentary (Cultural Anthropology) **LISTENING 2: High-Tech Nomads** A Radio Interview (Business)	• Recognize attitudes • Recognize meaning conveyed by intonation patterns • Predict content • Listen for main ideas • Listen for details	• Paraphrase • Speak about future plans and conditions • Conduct an interview • Take notes to prepare for a presentation or group discussion	• Phrasal verbs • Assess your prior knowledge of vocabulary
2 Global Cooperation **Q What does it mean to be a global citizen?** **LISTENING 1: The Campaign to Humanize the Coffee Trade** A Radio Report (Business) **LISTENING 2: The UN Global Compact** A Report (Economics)	• Organize notes with a T-chart • Listen for problems and solutions • Listen for numbers • Predict content • Listen for main ideas • Listen for details	• Cite sources • Use numbers in presentations • Practice stress and intonation patterns in quoting directly from sources • Take notes to prepare for a presentation or group discussion	• Collocations • Assess your prior knowledge of vocabulary
3 Size and Scale **Q Is bigger always better?** **LISTENING 1: Small Is the New Big** A Book Chapter (Business Management) **LISTENING 2: Sizing Up Colleges: One Size Does Not Fit All** A Podcast (Education)	• Listen for pros and cons • Listen for a speaker's attitudes • Listen for word stress and determine its impact on meaning • Predict content • Listen for main ideas • Listen for details	• Develop interview skills • Develop skills for answering interview questions • Take notes to prepare for a presentation or group discussion	• Connotations • Assess your prior knowledge of vocabulary
4 Alternative Thinking **Q Where do new ideas come from?** **LISTENING 1: Alternative Ideas in Medicine** Radio Reports (Public Health) **LISTENING 2: Boulder Bike-to-School Program Goes International** A Radio Interview (Recreation and Fitness)	• Use a table to organize note-taking • Distinguish between facts and opinions • Predict content • Listen for main ideas • Listen for details	• Use formal and informal language • Practice persuading listeners to accept a new idea • Take notes to prepare for a presentation or group discussion	• Idioms and informal expressions • Assess your prior knowledge of vocabulary

GRAMMAR	PRONUNCIATION	CRITICAL THINKING	UNIT OUTCOME
• Gerunds and infinitives	• Consonant variations	• Infer a speaker's attitudes • Hypothesize reasons why someone's attitudes changed • Assess your prior knowledge of content • Relate personal experiences to listening topics • Integrate information from multiple sources	• Interview a classmate and report on that person's attitudes concerning change.
• Reported speech	• Linking with final consonants	• Draw conclusions from pictures • Associate problems with solutions • Assess your prior knowledge of content • Relate personal experiences to listening topics • Integrate information from multiple sources	• Identify and report on aspects of a global problem.
• Parallel structure	• Word stress patterns	• Sort items into groups • Assess the usefulness of pieces of information • Assess your prior knowledge of content • Relate personal experiences to listening topics • Integrate information from multiple sources	• Role-play interviews for a job or a school and be prepared to answer a question that is creative or unusual.
• Noun clauses	• Reduced sounds in conditional modals—affirmative and negative	• Identify personal thought processes • Evaluate the factual basis of ideas • Assess your prior knowledge of content • Relate personal experiences to listening topics • Integrate information from multiple sources	• Develop a marketing presentation designed to sell a new invention or idea.

UNIT 1

Change

LISTENING ● recognizing attitudes
VOCABULARY ● phrasal verbs
GRAMMAR ● gerunds and infinitives
PRONUNCIATION ● consonant variations
SPEAKING ● paraphrasing

LEARNING OUTCOME

Interview a classmate and report on that person's attitudes concerning change.

Unit QUESTION

How do people react to change?

PREVIEW THE UNIT

A **Discuss these questions with your classmates.**

How many times has your family moved? Have you or your family moved for work, education, or other reasons?

List a few major changes in your life. Are you a person who welcomes new opportunities or one who avoids change?

Look at the photo. How is this an example of someone reacting to change?

B **Discuss the Unit Question above with your classmates.**

Listen to Level 10(CM), Track 1 to hear other answers.

C **According to recent United Nations statistics, people are migrating more than ever. Look at the statistics and discuss the question.**

Percentage of population that are immigrants:		Actual numbers of immigrants in specific region:	
United States	13	Western Asia	22 million
Canada	18.9	North America	45 million
Australia	19.6	Europe	64 million

Do these statistics surprise you? In a group, discuss why you think people move so often.

D **Read this blog post written by a university student who moved from China to Canada as a child. Then work in a group. Discuss the questions below.**

Good News, Bad News

By Huang Yubin Wednesday, May 5 at 11:22 a.m.

In China, we have a story about a farmer whose theme is "Good news, bad news—who knows?" What we sometimes think is bad news may turn out to be good news. When my parents decided to move to Canada, I was angry. I was just 12 years old. We lived in a big house with all of our family around us. I was considered a good student in my school, and I had lots of friends. I was a ping-pong champion and spent weekends playing with friends or competing in tournaments. Suddenly, my parents wanted me to give up the life I loved. Bad news.

I hated my new life. Even though I had studied English in my home country, I felt lost. My accent made it hard for people to understand me, and everyone spoke so fast I could barely understand them. I had to work twice as hard, and I was still not considered a good student. I made it worse by staying by myself; I didn't have any friends. I was a very unhappy person.

Looking back today, I wonder when all the bad news changed to good news. I am now at a prestigious university. I play on a club ping-pong team and have more friends than I have time for. I speak perfect English, and my parents are proud of me. When I graduate, I'll be able to take care of them. The change has done me good, and I'll probably stay where I am.

Comments (2) | Write a Comment | Email to a Friend

PREVIOUS REVIEW NEXT REVIEW

1. Would you consider a move like the one described here as good news or bad news? Why do you think the writer's feeling about his situation eventually changed?
2. Do you want to live and work in the same city where you were born?
3. Have you always had the same plan for your future career, or has it changed?

LISTENING

LISTENING 1 | The Reindeer People

VOCABULARY

Here are some words from Listening 1. Read the paragraphs. Then write each bold word next to the correct definition. (One definition under each paragraph will not be used.)

Some people feel sorry for groups of **nomads**. They must change environments during different times of the year in order to make sure their animals have enough food. It is not easy for outsiders to understand how these people feel close to their animals, the land, and nature. However, these groups choose not to **settle** in one place, despite government threats to remove any financial **subsidies** they receive that help them continue their lifestyle. With each new cycle of nature, nomadic tribes pack up and move on to a different area to **sustain** their herds of animals—and their way of life.

1. ________________ *(v.)* to make a place your permanent home
2. ________________ *(n.)* money provided to help individuals or groups reduce costs of services or goods
3. ________________ *(n.)* members of a community that moves with its animals from place to place
4. ________________ *(v.)* to provide enough of what somebody or something needs in order to live or exist
5. ________________ *(v.)* to develop or create a close relationship or connection with somebody or something

The 21st century will be a **critical** time for nomads and other indigenous groups. While the **elders** feel an **obligation** to preserve their customs and rituals and keep the beliefs of the culture alive, some members of the younger generation are ready to **embrace** change.

6. ________________ *(adj.)* extremely important because a future situation will be affected by it
7. ________________ *(n.)* something which you must do

8. ________________ *(n.)* stories from ancient times, especially one that was told to explain natural events to describe the early history of a people

9. ________________ *(n.)* older people, usually with a special status

10. ________________ *(v.)* to accept an idea or proposal with enthusiasm

> Many of these young people **contemplate** how different life would be if they went away to college or moved to a city to get a job and **make a living**. It's not that they dream of an **elite** lifestyle; they just don't want to **cope** with the hardships their parents endured.

11. ________________ *(v.)* to deal successfully with a difficult matter

12. ________________ *(v.)* to think about whether you should do something, or how you should do it

13. ________________ *(adj.)* unnecessarily expensive; more costly that the value of the object

14. ________________ *(adj.)* powerful, influential; wealthy or of high status

15. ________________ *(v.)* to earn money to buy the things you need

PREVIEW LISTENING 1

The Reindeer People

You are going to listen to a radio documentary, *The Reindeer People*, produced for the nonprofit organization Worlds of Difference. It is about a nomadic group that travels around the regions of Mongolia in order to find food for their animals.

How do you think nomads would react to opportunities to settle down and give up their life as herders? Check (✓) your prediction.

☐ They would welcome the government's help to relocate.

☐ They would fight to maintain their traditional culture.

☐ They would want to keep their nomadic life for themselves, but encourage their children to change.

LISTEN FOR MAIN IDEAS

Level 10(CM)
Track 2

Listen to the report. Write short answers. Then discuss them with a partner.

1. What two worlds do the nomadic reindeer herders feel they are caught between?

____

____

2. In what ways have the nomads been fighting to preserve their culture?

____

____

3. Why does the elder Sanjeem not want to settle?

____

____

LISTEN FOR DETAILS

Level 10(CM)
Track 3

A. Read the sentences in Activity B. Listen again and use the T-chart to take notes on the details.

Traditional mongolian life	Facing changes

B. **Use your notes from Activity A to complete the sentences. Compare your answers with a partner.**

Traditional mongolian life

1. The reindeer eat ____________________.
2. There are ____________________ people living in Sanjeem's group in the Tiga region.
3. Some of the staples, or main foods, in the Tiga diet that reindeer provide are ____________________, ____________________, and ____________________.
4. Uyumbottom went to the government for support for the traditional culture by pleading for ____________________.

Facing changes

5. With the end of government subsidies, nomadic life was threatened because herders lost free ____________________ care for their reindeer.
6. Because of ____________________ and attacks by ____________________, the size of the reindeer herd is decreasing.
7. The biologist from Colorado works for the NGO called Itgel. In Mongolian, *itgel* means ____________________.

WHAT DO YOU THINK?

Discuss the questions in a group.

1. Why do you think some elders in many cultures resist change? Why do you think younger people embrace change?
2. What are some reasons others in Mongolia might think the nomads should settle in permanent homes?
3. Do you think that these Mongolian nomads will be able to survive in the 21st century? Why or why not?

Listening Skill | Recognizing attitudes

Intonation is a tool speakers can use to indicate their attitude or emotions without stating them directly.

It is useful to recognize common intonation patterns because people do not always express their true attitude or feeling through their words alone. You can use their intonation and tone of voice to make inferences about what they really mean.

Intonation pattern	This can convey . . .
flat mid-pitch, low fall	sadness, regret
varied pitch	excitement, interest, or pleasure
very high, rising pitch	disbelief or surprise
sharp rise with a sharp fall	disagreement or denial

Level 10(CM)
Track 4

Listen to the intonation and attitude in these examples.

1. **Sadness or regret**

   The future of the reindeer herders sounds pretty uncertain.

2. **Excitement or interest**

   The female nomads have a lot to say about this issue.

3. **Disbelief or surprise**

   The number of reindeer is decreasing?

4. **Disagreement or denial**

   Personally, I think the herders are going to survive.

Level 10(CM) Track 5

A. **Listen to the sentences. Check (✓) the box for the attitude you can infer.**

Sentence	Sadness	Excitement or interest	Disagreement	Disbelief or surprise
1	☐	☐	☐	☐
2	☐	☐	☐	☐
3	☐	☐	☐	☐
4	☐	☐	☐	☐
5	☐	☐	☐	☐
6	☐	☐	☐	☐
7	☐	☐	☐	☐
8	☐	☐	☐	☐

Level 10(CM) Track 6

B. **Listen to these statements from Listening 1 and Listening 2. Circle the best inference for each one. With a partner, discuss how you made your choice.**

1. a. The speaker feels that the world should respect the life the nomads have chosen, even if others cannot understand their choice to live such a difficult life.

b. The speaker feels the government should protect the nomads from the forces of nature that are ruining a culture that cannot survive.

c. The speaker feels that the nomads should settle in one place and adopt a western lifestyle.

2. a. The speaker admires and envies the members of the group he is describing.

b. The speaker seems surprised and fascinated by this group of frequent travelers.

c. The speaker criticizes the members of this group for wanting to travel so much.

LISTENING 2 | High-Tech Nomads

VOCABULARY

Here are some words from Listening 2. Read their definitions. Then complete each sentence.

accomplish *(v.)* to succeed in doing or completing something
attention span *(n.)* the length of time somebody can stay interested in something
breakthroughs *(n.)* important developments that may lead to an agreement or an achievement
evolved *(adj.)* advanced; developed from simple early forms
intrepid *(adj.)* brave; not afraid of danger or difficulties
irony *(n.)* the amusing or strange aspect of a situation that is very different from what you expect
marginal *(adj.)* not part of a main or important group or situation
mundane *(adj.)* not interesting or exciting; ordinary
payoff *(n.)* an advantage or award for something done
psyche *(n.)* the mind; deep feelings and attitudes
roots *(n.)* the feeling or connections that you have with a place because you have lived there or your family came from there
stability *(n.)* a state of being steady and unchanging

1. Labeling people according to their income level, ethnic background, or language risks making them seem like ________________ groups and can lead to discrimination.
2. Those who want to investigate their ________________ and learn about their culture often go back to the country where their parents were born.
3. Those who have signed up for a trip on a spaceship are certainly ________________ travelers.
4. Something about the human ________________ makes us need to define our own space.
5. Scientific ________________ such as high-tech devices or advanced medical treatments have the potential to improve our lives.

6. The parents felt the children needed more _________________ and didn't want to move from one city to another too frequently.

7. He found _________________ in the idea that the city dwellers thought they were giving freedom to the nomads by making them move to the city.

8. Once you know what you want to _________________, it is easier to plan your actions and set goals.

9. The _________________ for working so hard was that she earned enough money to buy a new computer.

10. Some people complain about _________________ jobs, but others like having a set, predictable routine, even if it gets boring after a while.

11. Traditional societies that resist change are sometimes considered to be less _________________ than those that are more concerned with modern technological advances.

12. People with a short _________________ jump from project to project so they don't get bored.

PREVIEW LISTENING 2

High-Tech Nomads

You are going to hear Rudy Maxa, host of the radio show *The Savvy Traveler,* interview reporter Joel Garreau about his research on a special group of businesspeople called *high-tech nomads.*

Check (✓) the descriptions you think would apply to a high-tech nomad.

- ☐ a self-employed businessperson
- ☐ a cyberspace traveler, rather than a plane traveler
- ☐ a worker who changes offices frequently
- ☐ a computer "geek"
- ☐ an employee who can't keep one job
- ☐ a worker who has an email address but no business address
- ☐ a businessperson who works from home

Listen for Main Ideas

Level 10(CM)
Track 7

Listen to the interview. Write short answers. Then discuss them with a partner.

1. How could you summarize Joel Garreau's description of the character of the high-tech nomad in one sentence?

____

____

2. According to Garreau, why do these business travelers choose this nomadic life?

____

____

3. What do high-tech nomads give up for their lifestyle?

____

____

4. Garreau asks, "If these guys are so plugged in, and they can communicate from anywhere, why bother to travel at all?" How does he answer his own question?

____

____

Listen for Details

Level 10(CM)
Track 8

Listen again. Check (✓) the details that are correct. Compare your answers with a partner.

☐ 1. Both men and women are members of this high-tech nomad group.

☐ 2. Some high-tech nomads have million-dollar incomes.

☐ 3. High-tech nomads have common jobs, but just do them in uncommon ways.

☐ 4. One high-tech device that these businesspeople no longer have use for is the cell phone.

☐ 5. Even though these nomads like to travel for business, most have one specific home where they spend weekends, do laundry, and get mail.

☐ 6. The woman who swims every day does so because she needs exercise after the long plane rides.

☐ 7. Garreau says he needs more stability than the high-tech nomads.

☐ 8. Some high-tech nomads take their families with them when they travel on business.

☐ 9. Garreau states that high-tech nomads have short attention spans.

☐ 10. Nomads hope that one day technology will be so advanced that they won't need face-to-face meetings.

WHAT DO YOU THINK?

A. Discuss the questions in a group.

1. What do the speakers seem to think of the high-tech nomads? Do you agree with them? Why or why not?
2. Do you have the type of personality required to be a high-tech nomad? Do you have any interest in that sort of lifestyle? Why or why not?
3. In what ways do you try to be "wired" to the outside world? How much has your use of high-tech devices changed your daily life?

B. Think about both Listening 1 and Listening 2 as you discuss the question.

The reports described changes in the world around us (e.g., a lack of resources; an increase in technology). What other changes in today's world can you think of that could change the way some groups of people live, work, or study?

Vocabulary Skill | Phrasal verbs

Phrasal verbs, made up of a verb followed by a **particle**, are a common type of collocation. The particle (usually a preposition or an adverb) following the verb changes the meaning. For example, *take on* does not have the same meaning as *take* or *take over*. Phrasal verbs are listed separately in learners' dictionaries and are marked with a symbol.

> **ˌtake sth/sb↔ˈon** **1** to decide to do something; to agree to be responsible for something or someone: *I can't take on any extra work.* ◆ *We're not taking on any new clients at present.* **2** (of a bus, plane, or ship) to allow someone or something to enter: *The bus stopped to take on more passengers.* ◆ *The ship took on more fuel at Freetown.*

Some phrasal verbs take an object. A phrasal verb is **separable** if the object can be placed between the verb and the particle (*take* something *on*) as well as after it (*take on* something).

That group **took over** the meeting and discussed their changes to the plan.
We had contemplated **taking** the new project **on**, but decided not to.
Taking it **on** would have been too much work.

Phrasal verbs are often less formal and more conversational than one-word verbs with a similar meaning.

We decided to *take on* the new project. = more informal
We decided to *undertake* the new project. = more formal

Over time, some phrasal verbs join together to become nouns; examples from Listening 2 include *breakthrough* and *payoff*.

A. **Use a dictionary to complete the phrasal verbs with particles from the box. Then write S if the phrasal verb is separable and I if it is inseparable.**

at	in
away	out
away	up
back	up
back	up on
down	up with

____ 1. give ______: to give something as a gift

____ 2. give ______: to stop trying to do something

____ 3. give ______: to return something to its owner

____ 4. keep ______ (something): to continue working or doing something

____ 5. keep ______: to avoid going near something or someone

____ 6. keep ______ ______: to stay in contact with someone; to stay informed about a situation

____ 7. pick ______: to choose or select something

____ 8. pick ______: to collect something

____ 9. pick ______ ______: to return to a point already discussed

____ 10. turn ______: to return the way you have come

____ 11. turn ______: to reject or refuse something

____ 12. turn ______: to go to bed / go to sleep

B. **Complete the sentences with a phrasal verb from Activity A. If the verb is separable, rewrite the sentences using a pronoun. If the verb is not separable, put an *X* on the line.**

The group submitted an application for a government subsidy, but unfortunately, the government ___turned down___ the application.

___The government turned it down.___

1. It's important to ____________ from the edge of the cliff. You could fall!

   ____

2. I know that it's unhealthy to consume a lot of sugar, so I'm trying to ____________ soda.

   ____

3. High-tech nomads have no central place to ____________ their mail.

   ____

4. I'm not sure I understand what you mean. Can we ____________ the point you raised earlier about subsidies?

   ____

5. It's getting very late. I'm going to ____________ soon.

   ____

6. If you receive something you can't use and don't want, I think it's OK to ____________ that item ____________.

   ____

SPEAKING

Grammar | Gerunds and infinitives

Gerunds are formed by verb + *-ing*.

Infinitives are formed by *to* + base form of the verb.

Gerunds and infinitives are both nouns, even though they may look like verbs. They take the same position in a sentence as other nouns, such as subjects, direct objects, and objects of prepositional phrases.

1. Both gerunds and infinitives can be used as sentence subjects; this can make a sentence seem more formal.
2. Both gerunds and infinitives are used as direct objects; whether you use a gerund or an infinitive sometimes depends on the main verb in the sentence.
3. Only gerunds can be used as objects of prepositional phrases.
4. Gerunds are used as objects of verb phrases with *have* + noun.
5. Infinitives are also used in sentences whose subjects are noun phrases with *It* + adjective.

Study the examples in the chart.

	Infinitive	Gerund
1. Subject	**To meet people face-to-face** is important.	**Meeting people face-to-face** is important.
2. Object	High-tech nomads like **to meet people face-to-face.**	High-tech nomads like **meeting people face-to-face.**
3. Object of a prepositional phrase	✗	He is interested in **meeting people face-to-face.**
4. Object of a verb phrase with *have* + noun	✗	He has difficulty **meeting people face-to-face.**
5. Object of a noun phrase with *it* + adjective	It is important **to meet people face-to-face.**	✗

Here are some common verbs and phrases that are followed by gerunds or infinitives.

	Infinitive	Gerund
avoid, dislike, enjoy, finish, mind, practice, quit		✓
agree, decide, expect, force, hope, intend, plan, promise	✓	
continue, hate, like, love, prefer, start	✓	✓
have difficulty/fun/a problem/a hard time/trouble		✓
it is easy/hard/important/necessary	✓	

A. Complete each sentence with the gerund or infinitive form of the verb in parentheses. Check your answers with a partner. In some cases, more than one answer is possible.

1. Many Mongolian nomads would prefer ________________ (maintain) their traditional lifestyle.
2. It appears that the Mongolian nomads don't have trouble ________________ (move) as the seasons change.
3. Mongolia's geography forces people ________________ (embrace) the nomadic life.
4. Still, it is not easy ________________ (cope) with so many changes.
5. High-tech nomads avoid ________________ (stay) in any one place or job for too long.
6. They don't have a problem ________________ (use) an airport as their office.
7. Some of them intend ________________ (travel) for just a few years, and others choose it for their entire career.

Tip for Success

Learners' dictionaries list object forms needed after main verbs. If you look up *deny*, you'll see *doing sth*, so you know the verb that follows *deny* should use the gerund form: *He denied* ***taking*** *it.*

B. Work with a partner. Discuss the questions. Use verbs and expressions from the chart followed by gerunds and infinitives.

1. Think about your life now and then how it might change in the future. What do you enjoy doing now? What do you dislike doing? What do you intend to change in the future? What are some things you hope to do?

2. Think about a career you are interested in. Do you hope to get a job in that field? How do you plan to prepare or train for that? Will it be easy or difficult to find a job? Could it be necessary to move to another city or country? Would you mind moving?

Pronunciation | Consonant variations

As you've learned, vowel sounds may change according to their position in a word and the other sounds around them. **Consonant sounds** may also change. This chart summarizes some of the important variations in English consonant sounds.

Level 10(CM) Track 9

Listen to and repeat the examples.

Consonant variation	Explanation	Conditions	Examples
Aspiration of /p/, /t/, /k/	add an extra puff of air after the voiceless sounds /p/, /t/, /k/	when /p/, /t/, /k/ come at the beginning of a stressed syllable (except when preceded by *s*)	*poor* *appeal* *tech* *return* *cope* *account*
Flap or tap /t̬/	use a quick flick or tap /t̬/ of the tongue on the roof of the mouth for *t* and *d*	when a *t* or *d* comes between a stressed vowel and an unstressed vowel (American English)	*leader* *matter* *subsidy*
Palatalization	pronounce *d* like/ʤ/ and *t* like /tʃ/, creating friction rather than a stop	when *d* or *t* combines with a following /y/ sound	*question* *nature* *situate* *gradual*

Level 10(CM)
Track 10

A. Listen to these pairs of words and repeat them.

1. Feel the extra puff of air with your hand when you say the second word in each pair.
   open – opinion
   atom – atomic
   intern – turn

2. Feel how the quick tap /ţ/ is substituted for /t/ or /d/ in the second word in each pair.
   master – matter
   lender – leader
   invitation – invited

3. Feel how your tongue creates friction with the roof of your mouth in the second word instead of just stopping the sound.
   grader – gradual
   native – natural
   captive – capture

Level 10(CM)
Track 11

B. Circle the three words in each set that have these features. Then listen and check your answers.

1. aspirated /p/
   a. cope　　b. expand　　c. payoff　　d. policy

2. aspirated /k/
   a. connection　　b. crazy　　c. accomplish　　d. cycle

3. aspirated /t/
   a. routine　　b. elite　　c. attention　　d. tourist

4. flap /ţ/
   a. critical　　b. material　　c. ability　　d. letter

5. flap /ţ/
   a. media　　b. pleaded　　c. nomadic　　d. advisor

6. palatalized /tʃ/
   a. century　　b. future　　c. fifty　　d. culture

7. palatalized /dʒ/
   a. gradual　　b. reindeer　　c. schedule　　d. individual

Level 10(CM)
Track 12

C. Listen to these sentences and circle the words with an aspirated, flap, or palatalized *t*.

Welcome to the world of the high-tech nomad. Writer Joel Garreau investigated this unique breed of traveler for *The Washington Post*, and he sat down with us recently to tell us what he learned.

Speaking Skill | Paraphrasing

To **paraphrase** is to repeat an idea in a way that keeps the same meaning but uses different words. Speakers paraphrase for emphasis, or to make a meaning clearer or easier to understand. Sometimes we paraphrase what we have heard a speaker say just to clarify our own understanding.

Level 10(CM)
Track 13

Listen to the way the Rudy Maxa paraphrases some of Joel Garreau's words in his interview.

> Garreau: One of the great ironies of this lifestyle is that, you know, you ask yourself, well if these guys are so plugged in, and they can communicate from anywhere, **why bother travel at all**?
>
> Maxa: Exactly. **Why do you even move?**

Here, Maxa shows that he has understood the question that Garreau is asking; also, by repeating it, he emphasizes the question for the listening audience.

Here are some techniques that you can use to paraphrase.

> Original sentence: Discovering the nomads was a surprising experience for us.

Use synonyms

> Paraphrase: The reporter said that finding the nomads was an astonishing experience.

Vary word forms

> Paraphrase: The discovery of the nomadic group surprised them.

Change positive to negative forms

> Paraphrase: The discovery of the nomads was not expected.

When paraphrasing, it is also common to:

Combine sentences and ideas

Original sentences: We were at least listened to. . . I'm encouraged by this.

Paraphrase: Uyumbotton said that she felt encouraged because at least the government listened to them.

Break a long idea or sentence into two

Original sentence: Mongolia's geography, a boundless wilderness with soil that can't sustain agriculture, forces people to embrace the nomadic life.

Paraphrase: The narrator explains that Mongolia has vast lands, but it is impossible to grow food there. As a result, a nomadic life is necessary.

When paraphrasing in a conversation, use expressions such as *in other words, what I'm/you're saying is . . ., so what I/you mean is . . . .*

A. Listen to your partner read a sentence below. Paraphrase the sentence using the techniques in the Speaking Skill box. Ask your partner to confirm that you paraphrased the ideas accurately.

A: *These guys tend to have very short attention spans on average.*

B: *So you mean most high-tech nomads don't have long attention spans?*

A: *Yes, exactly / Yes, that's right / Indeed.*

1. The economic advisor to Mongolia's president did not have encouraging words.

2. And the great irony is that the reason they are nomads is for face-to-face contact.

3. Well it's only been in the last ten years that we've had enough wired technology to make this barely possible.

4. When Mongolia's communist government was toppled by a democratic revolution in the 1990s, his state salary was withdrawn.

Tip for Success

Even when you paraphrase another person's ideas, it is still necessary to give credit to the person.

B. **Work with a partner. Role-play a conversation between one of the people in the recordings and an interviewer who paraphrases the speaker's words.**

A: Mr. Garreau, do you believe that high-tech nomads are crazy?

B: No, I couldn't live that nomadic lifestyle, but these people are successful.

A: In other words, even though the life of a nomad isn't for you, their success shows that they aren't crazy.

Possible topics:

Ask Sanjeem what would happen if his people moved closer to the city.

Ask Sanjeem's wife why she went to the capital or what the results of the trip were.

Ask Sanjeem's granddaughter about the songs she sings.

Ask Dyson why she swims every day.

Ask Garreau what he thinks high-tech nomads miss most.

Ask Maxa what he learned from his interview with Garreau.

Unit Assignment | Conduct a personal interview

In this section, you will interview a classmate to find out whether she or he resists or embraces change and then report on your findings. As you prepare your presentation, think about the Unit Question, "How do people react to change?" and refer to the Self-Assessment checklist on page 26.

For alternative unit assignments, see the *Q: Skills for Success Teacher's Handbook*.

CONSIDER THE IDEAS

The topic of change has fascinated many great thinkers, writers, and leaders. In a group, read and discuss the following quotations about change. Take turns paraphrasing the ideas and explaining your reactions to them. Which ones seem positive? Which are negative?

Famous Quotations about Change

Change is the law of life. And those who look only to the past or present are certain to miss the future. - John Kennedy, American president

There is nothing like returning to a place that remains unchanged to find how you yourself have altered. - Nelson Mandela, South African president

Certain things should stay the way they are. You ought to be able to stick them in one of those big glass cases and just leave them alone.
- Holden Caulfield in *Catcher in the Rye*, by J. D. Salinger, American novelist

Only the wisest and stupidest of men never change.
- Confucius, Chinese philosopher

Everything is in a process of change, nothing endures; we do not seek permanence. - Masatoshi Naito, Japanese artist

You can clutch the past so tightly to your chest that it leaves your arms too full to embrace the present. - Jan Glidewell, American journalist

To change and to change for the better are two different things.
- German proverb

Any change, even a change for the better, is always accompanied by drawbacks and discomforts. - Arnold Bennett, English novelist

That's the risk you take if you change: that people you've been involved with won't like the new you. But other people who do will come along.
- Lisa Alther, American novelist

Prepare and Speak

Tip Critical Thinking

In Activity A, you have to discuss the quotations and **defend** your ideas by giving explanations for your opinions. When you defend your opinions, you use your own personal values and beliefs.

A. GATHER IDEAS Follow these steps to prepare for your interview.

1. Work with a partner. Discuss the quotations above. Explain why you agree or disagree with them.
2. In your notebook, write seven questions that will help you find out how your partner reacts to change. Your questions can cover different areas including changes in family, school, careers, traditions, or reactions to the people in the recordings.

Tip for Success

In a conversation, it is important to have good eye contact so the speaker knows you are listening and interested in what he or she is saying.

B. ORGANIZE IDEAS Interview your partner, and take notes on his or her responses to your questions in Activity A. Then ask your partner to choose one of the quotations from Consider the Ideas and explain why it best fits his or her attitude toward change.

	Partner's Responses
Quotation	
Explanation	

C. SPEAK Summarize what you found out about your partner's attitudes toward change in a presentation to the class. Use your partner's favorite quotation as an introduction or a conclusion. Refer to the Self-Assessment checklist below before you begin.

CHECK AND REFLECT

A. CHECK Think about the Unit Assignment as you complete the Self-Assessment checklist.

SELF-ASSESSMENT		
Yes	No	
☐	☐	I was able to speak fluently about the topic.
☐	☐	My partner and class understood me.
☐	☐	I used phrasal verbs correctly and in appropriate situations.
☐	☐	I used gerunds and infinitives correctly and in a variety of sentence positions.
☐	☐	I pronounced consonants correctly.
☐	☐	I paraphrased to emphasize and to clarify understanding.

B. REFLECT Discuss these questions with a partner.

What is something new you learned in this unit?

Q Look back at the Unit Question. Is your answer different now than when you started this unit? If yes, how is it different? Why?

Track Your Success

Circle the words and phrases you learned in this unit.

Nouns
attention span
breakthrough
elder
irony
nomad
obligation
payoff
psyche
roots
stability AWL
subsidy AWL

Verbs
accomplish
contemplate
cope 🔑
embrace
evolve
settle 🔑
sustain AWL

Phrasal Verbs
give away 🔑
give back
give up 🔑
keep at
keep away from
keep up with
pick out
pick up 🔑
pick up on
turn back
turn down
turn in

Adjectives
critical 🔑
elite
evolved AWL
intrepid
marginal AWL
mundane

Phrase
make a living

🔑 Oxford 3000™ words
AWL Academic Word List

Check (✓) the skills you learned. If you need more work on a skill, refer to the page(s) in parentheses.

LISTENING	○ I can recognize attitudes. (p. 9)
VOCABULARY	○ I can use phrasal verbs. (p. 15)
GRAMMAR	○ I can use gerunds and infinitives. (pp. 18–19)
PRONUNCIATION	○ I can use consonant variations. (p. 20)
SPEAKING	○ I can paraphrase. (pp. 22–23)
LEARNING OUTCOME	○ I can interview a classmate and report on that person's attitudes concerning change.

UNIT 2

Global Cooperation

LISTENING ● organizing notes with a T-chart
VOCABULARY ● collocations
GRAMMAR ● reported speech
PRONUNCIATION ● linking with final consonants
SPEAKING ● citing sources

LEARNING OUTCOME

Identify and report on aspects of a global problem.

Unit QUESTION

What does it mean to be a global citizen?

PREVIEW THE UNIT

A **Discuss these questions with your classmates.**

Which of these concerns get the most attention: short-term disasters such as hurricane relief or long-term problems such as world hunger? Why?

Look at the photo. Have you or someone you know participated in an activity that reflects a desire to become a better global citizen?

B **Discuss the Unit Question above with your classmates.**

Listen to Level 10(CM), Track 14 to hear other answers.

C Look at the photos. What problems do you see? Talk with a partner and write your ideas. Then think of four more problems you think the world faces today.

Problems the world faces today

____

____

____

____

____

D Work with a group. For each problem in Activity C, decide who is primarily responsible for solving the problem. (There may be more than one answer.) Write the problem beside the correct heading.

Governments	
NGOs (non-governmental organizations)	
Businesses	
Individuals	

LISTENING

LISTENING 1 | The Campaign to Humanize the Coffee Trade

VOCABULARY

Here are some words from Listening 1. Read the sentences. Then write each bold word next to the correct definition.

1. Many celebrity **activists** worked together to bring attention to the effects of the tsunami and to raise money for countries affected by it.
2. If a local community effort, or grassroots campaign, gets a lot of media attention, it might **transform** into a national or even a global fight for change.
3. Many farmers are forced to find other jobs because they cannot **afford** the high costs of producing food.
4. Some businesspeople who like risk base their investments on **speculation** and luck rather than on past performance history.
5. There was a **massive** demand for sugar, but because of agricultural problems, the supply was very low.
6. Water is a basic **commodity** that is scarce in many parts of the world.
7. The grower sells his product to a **processor**, who then gets it ready for the market.
8. Human rights groups spend a lot of their energy trying to **devise** ways to improve labor laws around the world.
9. **Roughly** 884 million people worldwide have unsafe drinking water, and according to the humanitarian group Save the Children, this estimate is low.
10. In order to avoid the obstacles that can prevent small businesses from succeeding, some people prefer to join a **co-op** and work together with other small business owners.
11. The United Nations Global Compact wants businesses to **guarantee** that they will reduce their environmental impact, not just say they hope it will happen.
12. The importer didn't have a license to do business in that country, so she needed an **intermediary** to buy the products for her.

a. ____________ (*n.*) the activity of buying and selling goods or shares in a company in the hope of making a profit, but with the risk of losing money

b. ____________ (*v.*) to change someone or something completely

c. ____________ (*adv.*) more or less; approximately

d. ____________ (*v.*) to give a promise

e. ____________ (*n.*) a product or raw material that can be bought and sold

f. ____________ (*n.*) someone who passes on information; a middleman

g. ____________ (*n.*) something or someone that changes materials before they are sold

h. ____________ (*v.*) to invent a plan or system

i. ____________ (*n.*) someone who wants to achieve political or social change

j. ____________ (*v.*) to be able to pay for something

k. ____________ (*adj.*) very big

l. ____________ (*n.*) a community organization of people working together towards a shared goal

PREVIEW LISTENING 1

The Campaign to Humanize the Coffee Trade

You are going to listen to a report, "The Campaign to Humanize the Coffee Trade," by Daniel Zwerdling for American RadioWorks. It addresses an issue of global concern for a product consumed in almost every country.

Check (✓) your predictions of what the speaker will say about *humanizing* the coffee trade, improving the conditions for the workers.

☐ Coffee production in small villages is usually not controlled by the farmers themselves.

☐ Products that come from socially responsible businesses that protect workers and the environment cost less because they come from small companies.

☐ Coffee farmers earn less than one-tenth of the money from their beans sold in other countries.

LISTEN FOR MAIN IDEAS

Level 10(CM)
Track 15

Listen to the report. Then write a sentence for each topic to express the main idea.

1. The lives and homes of the coffee farmers

____

____

2. The role of the coyote, or middleman

____

____

3. The goal of the Fair Trade system

____

____

LISTEN FOR DETAILS

Level 10(CM)
Track 16

A. Read the statements. Then listen again. Check (✓) the statements that are true according to the report.

☐ 1. The coffee farmers introduced here say they send their coffee into town on trucks.

☐ 2. The coyotes, or middlemen, buy the coffee beans for 50 cents or less a pound.

☐ 3. Zwerdling says that in Washington, D.C., he spends less than $9.00 a pound for coffee.

☐ 4. Coffee is not a highly traded commodity.

☐ 5. Fair Trade was started by Europeans.

☐ 6. At the time of the report, over 300 groups of farmers around the world had joined the Fair Trade system.

☐ 7. Large corporate plantations can join Fair Trade if they promise to follow fair business practices.

☐ 8. Guillermo Denaux explains that under Fair Trade, farmers are basically guaranteed to earn enough money for food, education, clothes, and health care.

B. **Who sells coffee to whom? Number the people in the order that they purchase coffee after the farmer offers it for sale. Then listen again and check your answers.**

____ a coffee shop

_1_ a coyote, or middleman

____ a processor

____ a roaster

____ the consumer

____ an exporter

WHAT DO YOU THINK?

Discuss the questions in a group.

1. Would you be willing to pay extra for Fair Trade products? Why or why not? How much more would you pay (than you do now) for a cup of coffee? A chocolate bar? A cotton T-shirt?
2. Zwerdling says that "consumers have to help, too." In what ways can consumers help in the development of the Fair Trade network?
3. Who should determine prices of luxury commodities (such as coffee or chocolate)? Who should determine the prices of necessities (such as vegetables)? What might happen if farmers were allowed to charge as much as they wanted for their products?

Listening Skill — Organizing notes with a T-chart

After you listen to a lecture, it's useful to **organize your notes**. This makes it easier to understand and remember the information and makes it easier to use your notes to write papers or study for tests.

Some lectures follow organizational patterns that are easily noted in a **T-chart**. Some common patterns include cause and effect, problem and solution, and discussions of differences before and after a particular event or time.

To use a T-chart, divide your paper into two columns and write one category at the top of each column. Write connected ideas across from each other; however, remember that there might be, for example, several effects from one cause or several problems for one solution. Drawing arrows can help you see the connections between ideas.

Level 10(CM)
Track 17

Listen to this excerpt from Listening 1, and see how a student noted the ideas in the chart:

Problems	Solutions
• Farmers are poor and powerless. • Farmers don't know who buys their coffee. • Many different people buy and sell the coffee beans before the consumer.	The Fair Trade system can help farmers earn more money and gain some power.

Remember that in a lecture, you might hear some of the information out of order. However, if you can note problems in the problem column and solutions in the solution column, you can reorder them later when you revise your notes. If you hear information that you don't have time to write down, draw a line; then you can ask your instructor or a classmate later. Sometimes your instructor might ask you to research the missing information or come up with your own ideas.

Level 10(CM)
Track 18

Listen to students talking about humanitarian organizations. Write the problems and solutions they discuss. Then compare notes with a partner.

Tip Critical Thinking

This activity asks you to **identify** the problems and solutions you hear the speakers talk about. Identifying ideas is one way to show you understand the information.

	Problems	Solutions
1.		
2.		
3.		
4.		

Clean drinking water is a precious commodity.

LISTENING 2 | The UN Global Compact

VOCABULARY

Tip for Success

These noun phrases are all collocations. The field of business has many noun phrases that are collocations. See the Vocabulary Skill on page 41 for more information on collocations.

Here are some words and phrases from Listening 2. Read the sentences. Then write each bold word or phrase next to the correct definition.

1. India is recognized as a key **emerging economy** in the world. There is some risk in investing there, but potential for enormous profits and growth, too.
2. Many organizations try to ensure that proper **labor standards** exist so that employees have safe conditions at their jobs.

3. Businesses worry about the **confidence of investors** because if people don't invest, there won't be money to innovate and expand, or perhaps even to stay in business.

4. Institutions such as the World Bank provide loans to developing countries to improve their **social impact** in the world.

a. ____________________________ laws that protect workers

b. ____________________________ the effects of an organization or agency on others

c. ____________________________ a region that is experiencing rapid growth and industrialization

d. ____________________________ a feeling or belief by people with money that it is safe to spend it in order to make a future profit

5. Businesses have easily identifiable assets, or property. They also have **intangible assets**, like a good reputation, that are not easily visible.

6. At the end of the year, a corporation's **accounting practices** might be examined to make sure the business reports are accurate and honest.

7. In tough economic times, families need to reduce unnecessary **household expenditures** such as eating in restaurants or going to the movies.

8. I am only interested in buying **ethical goods** for people as gifts this year. I don't want to support any businesses that don't treat workers fairly.

e. ____________________________ the costs of taking care of a home and family

f. ____________________________ methods of keeping financial records

g. ____________________________ products that are judged to be morally acceptable and not harmful to society or the workers who produce them

h. ____________________________ things of value that cannot be seen, such as knowledge

9. Even though countries want to **exploit** their own natural resources, they have to consider the environmental impact of using those resources too quickly.

10. In recent years, businesses have tried to find ways of being **proactive** with problems so they can take action before being criticized.

11. The principles, or basic beliefs, of a company determine its **core strategies**.

12. The country's economic policies are focused on creating a **sustainable market** to attract and keep foreign investors.

i. ______________________ a system that can operate continuously while still meeting global economic, environmental, and social needs

j. ______________________ to use something well in order to gain as much from it as possible

k. ______________________ controlling a situation by making things happen rather than waiting for things to happen and then reacting to them

l. ______________________ primary or fundamental plans of action for a business

The United Nations building

PREVIEW LISTENING 2

The UN Global Compact

The United Nations, itself a symbol of international cooperation, has many subgroups that work in specific areas. You are going to listen to a report on the UN Global Compact. The report discusses a special formal agreement, or compact, among businesses around the world on the issues that concern them.

Check (✓) the issues you expect to hear discussed in the report.

- ☐ corruption
- ☐ import and export prices
- ☐ pollution
- ☐ treatment of employees
- ☐ investor confidence
- ☐ worker safety
- ☐ climate change
- ☐ consumer spending

Listen for Main Ideas

Level 10(CM)
Track 19

Listen to the report on the Global Compact. Circle the answer that best completes each statement.

1. The *Exxon Valdez* disaster and the Enron collapse showed that businesses
   a. can act responsibly without regulations.
   b. are guilty of corporate irresponsibility.
2. Expansion into the global market brings more risk to the public because
   a. emerging markets have weaker regulations.
   b. emerging markets will increase competition.
3. In order to participate in the UN Global Compact, companies must promise to
   a. take responsibility for their own actions.
   b. report irresponsible actions by other businesses.
4. Two of the ten areas that the Global Compact is intended to safeguard are
   a. labor standards and business reputations.
   b. human rights and the environment.
5. Evidence of changes in public attitudes includes findings that people are
   a. spending more money on ethical goods.
   b. more concerned about the cost of a product than the reputation of the company that produced it.
6. Ban Ki-Moon's hopes for the future of the Global Compact include
   a. limiting global expansion and development.
   b. creating sustainable markets.

LISTEN FOR DETAILS

Level 10(CM)
Track 20

Read this list of supporting details. Then listen again. Complete the chart with the correct numbers as you listen. Check your answers with a partner.

Details	Numbers
1. The year of the *Exxon Valdez* disaster	
2. The number of gallons of crude oil spilled into the water by the *Exxon Valdez*	
3. The number of dollars in foreign direct investment at the time of this report	
4. The year the UN started the Global Compact	
5. The number of Global Compact principles the participating companies agree to uphold	
6. The percentage of a company's market value that is determined by its reputation and intangible assets	
7. The share price of Enron before its bad reputation caused the price to fall to less than 50 cents	
8. The percentage of CEOs who report doing more now to incorporate environmental, social, and political issues into their core strategies	
9. The number of companies in the Global Compact when it first started	
10. The number of countries in the Global Compact at the time of this report	

WHAT DO YOU THINK?

A. Discuss the questions in a group.

1. What do you think are the most serious problems caused by businesses and corporations that the Global Compact should force them to address?
2. Do you think corporations that follow the Global Compact are motivated more by the desire for profits, the desire to be better global citizens, or something else?
3. What are some examples you've seen of efforts by businesses or individuals to be better global citizens?

B. **Think about both Listening 1 and Listening 2 as you discuss the questions.**

1. Did the two recordings change your mind about global citizenship and cooperation, or did they confirm views you already had? In what ways?
2. What are some current problems that would benefit from global solutions on a small scale or a grassroots level?

Vocabulary Skill Collocations

To increase your fluency and expand your vocabulary, it is important to know about **collocation**, or the way two or more words are commonly combined when written or spoken. Compound words, idioms, lexical phrases, and phrasal verbs, as well as adjective-noun combinations, are examples of collocations.

Collocations are based on common usage and not usually on grammatical rules.

We say . . .	but not . . .
crude oil	rough oil
Fair Trade products	Kind Trade products
climb the corporate ladder	climb the business ladder

Learners' and collocations dictionaries are good tools for finding out which word collocates with another. A thesaurus might lead you in the wrong direction, however, because even though two words are synonyms, they will probably not collocate with the same words.

Synonyms	global	international
Collocations	global warming	international borders

Tip for Success

One way to check for common collocations is to use the Internet to search for a phrase in quotations. For example, "emerging market" gives over two million hits, but "emerging economy" fewer than 200,000.

A. **Choose the phrase that has the correct collocation. Check a collocations dictionary if necessary.**

1. Agencies like Amnesty International help protect (personal rights / human rights) around the world.
2. We need to write the (final draft / end draft) of our proposal.
3. The (prices rose / prices ascended) when the corporation took over.
4. They carried the coffee (down and up / up and down) the mountain.
5. The (short supply of / little supply of) that commodity affected prices.

6. My favorite charity is one that brings (disaster comfort / disaster relief) to victims of hurricanes.

7. We need to (make some research / do some research) on that project before we invest in it.

8. (Startup markets / Emerging markets) are those in developing countries where businesses see the possibility for growth and are making new investments.

9. The (coffee shop / coffee store) bought most of its coffee from Fair Trade organizations.

10. Businesses that abuse the environment are partly responsible for the problem of (weather change / climate change).

B. Work with a partner. Circle the two words or phrases that collocate with the bold word or expression. Check a learners' or collocations dictionary if necessary.

1. **business**	a. run a . . .	b. make a . . .	c. go into . . .
2. **money**	a. make . . .	b. spend . . .	c. afford . . .
3. **costs**	a. get rid of . . .	b. run up . . .	c. cover . . .
4. **confidence**	a. grow . . . in	b. have. . . in	c. lose. . . in
5. **responsibility**	a. take . . . for	b. discover . . . for	c. have . . . for
6. **chief . . . officer**	a. financial	b. executive	c. management

C. With your partner, write at least six sentences using collocations from Activity B.

____

____

____

____

____

____

SPEAKING

Grammar Reported speech

In **reported speech** (or indirect speech), you restate what someone else has said or written. It is often used to incorporate information from another source into a presentation. In reported speech, it is important to keep the same meaning as the original source, although it is not necessary to use the exact words.

Reported speech	Examples
requires a backshift in verb tense when talking about things said in and about the past simple present → simple past present continuous → past continuous simple past → present perfect present perfect → past perfect *will* → *would* *can* → *could* *may* → *might*	The farmer said, "We need to get a higher price." The farmer said that **they needed** to get a higher price. The board said, "We will invest more in emerging markets in the future." The board said **they would invest** more in emerging markets.
keeps the same verb tense if the speaker's words involve a timeless or current situation or event	He said, "Climate change is a reality." He said (that) climate change **is** a reality.
uses statement word order, even if the original source is a question	The executive asked, "What's the agenda?" The executive asked **what the agenda was.**
starts with a reporting verb such as *say*, *tell*, *ask*, *add*, *assert*, *point out*, *state*, *remark*, *respond*, and *warn* has an optional *that* for statements	"The environmental crisis is a global problem." (Barry Commoner) Barry Commoner **asserts (that)** the environmental crisis is a global problem.
may require a change in pronoun from *I/we/you* to clarify the reporter's relationship to what is said	I told her, "You and I can do more." I told her **she and I** could do more.
uses *if* or *whether* to introduce a *Yes/No* question, or an infinitive to introduce a command	The UN speaker asked, "Are you ready to make a global commitment? Then do it." The UN speaker asked **whether** they were ready to make a global commitment and told them **to do** it.

A. **Work with a partner and take turns. One person reads the quotation, and the other changes it to reported speech. Remember to begin with a reporting verb.**

1. The farmer, about growing coffee: "It's a lot of work, and sometimes we can't even cover our costs."

   The farmer stated that growing coffee was a lot of work, and . . .

2. Deborah Amos, to the radio audience: "Do you ever think about the farmers who grew that coffee?"

3. Georg Kell, about the Global Compact: "Initially we started off with a moral core."

4. Ban Ki-Moon, UN Secretary General: "Together we can achieve a new face of globalization."

5. Dan Zwerdling, about the coffee farmers: "These farmers are the poorest and most powerless part of the global coffee trade."

6. Daniel Zwerdling, about Fair Trade: "Still, the Fair Trade network can't raise all the money that farmers need just by cutting out middlemen. Consumers have to help, too."

B. **Work in a group. Sit in a circle. Share a fact or ask a question about a global issue. The person to your right will report what you said and then add another fact or question. Continue around the circle until everyone has had a chance to share and report.**

A: In Cambodia last year, heavy rains caused flooding, and many farmers' crops were destroyed.

B: Student A reported that in Cambodia last year, heavy rains had caused flooding and many crops had been destroyed. Do any international organizations help farmers in different countries?

C: Student B asked if any international organizations help farmers in different countries. I think the United Nations . . .

Pronunciation | Linking with final consonants

In order to improve fluency, it is important to connect the final sound of one word or syllable to the initial sound of the next, especially in the same thought group. If you say each sound perfectly, but in isolation, your speech will sound unnatural.

It is important not to drop final consonants, or your speech will be unclear because one word may be confused with another. *Time is money* should *not* sound like *Tie is money*.

Do not link a word that ends with a consonant to one that begins with another consonant by inserting a vowel sound between them. This will cause you to add an extra syllable that will confuse your listener. *The date began with a three* should *not* sound like *The data began with a three*.

Level 10(CM) Track 21

Read the principles of linking with final consonants and study the examples in the chart. Then listen to the example sentences.

Principles of linking	Examples
1. Join a final consonant sound to the vowel sound at the beginning of the next word.	They sol**d** items ma**de** in Africa thousand**s** of mile**s** away.
2. When the same consonant ends one word and begins the next, do not insert a vowel sound. Hold the consonant longer instead of repeating it.	They wan**t** to ta**ke** control of production.
3. When a word ends in the consonant sounds *t*, *k*, *d*, *p*, *g*, or *b*, do not release the first sound, but say the second one right away.	They grow some of the bes**t** **c**offee you can drink.

Level 10(CM) Track 22

A. Link the final consonants in these phrases. Write ‿ where the sounds are joined, ___ where the same sound is held longer, and) where the final consonant sound is not released. Then listen and repeat to check your work. Practice saying the phrases aloud with a partner.

1. an economist
2. growing coffee
3. special label
4. stuck in poverty
5. can't cover costs
6. basic commodity
7. household expenditure
8. global expansion
9. climate change
10. environmental issues

B. Mark the places where sounds should be linked. Then ask and answer the questions with a partner. Help each other improve linking sounds by listening carefully and pointing out problems.

1. What time is the conference on the global economy?
2. What kind of help does a refugee camp provide?
3. How can countries demonstrate international unity?
4. What are some ways to help earthquake victims?
5. How can companies promise to reduce their environmental impact?
6. What are some nonprofit organizations that collect food donations for the hungry?
7. What are some ways you take care of the people in your community?
8. How might an economist describe fair trade?

Speaking Skill | Citing sources

When giving academic presentations, you need to tell the audience where your information comes from. Giving credit to authorities or outside sources will make your presentation more believable and informative. You can show that you have studied background information and up-to-date material.

In speaking, you can cite information by:

- introducing the person who wrote or said something important about your topic.
- telling where and when it was published or said.
- using reported speech to restate the speaker's idea.

When citing a speaker's words from a specific point in the past, related to past activities or ideas, use a reporting verb in the past form (he *stated*, she *explained*, they *claimed*).

When citing written material, a quotation that is closely related in time to the speaker, or a statement of a universally accepted idea, it is common to use either the present perfect form (*he has asserted*) or the citational present (*the report proves*; *research shows*).

Here are some common phrases for citing sources:

According to X, . . .
As X says / explains / reports, . . .
X's article shows . . .
In [year], X proved that . . .
In a survey published in [year], the results showed . . .
At a conference on [date], X explained how . . .

A. Add a different opening for each sentence to introduce the source provided in parentheses. Read your sentences to a partner and compare your choices.

1. ______________________________ Fair Trade is a social movement that has been organized to give power to developing countries. (Wikipedia)

2. ______________________________ 200,000 people attended a series of Live 8 concerts in London's Hyde Park to combat poverty in Africa. (BBC News, July 3, 2005)

3. ______________________________ the Heifer Foundation has provided an orphanage in Vietnam with an animal farm, so children learn how to raise and care for animals. (Rose Tran Bach Yen, orphanage director, Vietnam)

4. ______________________________ more than 90 percent of CEOs are doing more about environmental, social, and political issues now. (2007, McKinsey survey)

Tip for Success

Try to use a variety of reporting verbs or phrases, and don't always use them at the beginning of a sentence. For example: *The New York Fair Trade Day this year was an enormous success,* ***according to Scott Codey.*** *The interest in buying Fair Trade products for gifts,* ***Codey added,*** *increases every year.*

5. ______________________________ "My fellow Americans, people all over the world, we need to solve the climate crisis. It's not a political issue; it's a moral issue." (Al Gore, Academy Award acceptance speech, February 2007)

6. ______________________________ colleagues at Doctors Without Borders treated more than 150,000 children suffering from hunger around the world. (Susan Shepherd, pediatrician, *The New York Times*, January 30, 2008)

B. Work with a partner. Read these descriptions of organizations that have made a difference. Take turns asking questions about them and citing the information.

1. Save the Children is the leading independent organization creating lasting change for children in need in the United States and around the world. For more than 75 years, Save the Children has been helping children survive and thrive by improving their health, education and economic opportunities and, in times of acute crisis, mobilizing rapid life-saving assistance to help children recover from the effects of war, conflict and natural disasters. (Save the Children, Causecast.org, http://www.causecast.org)

2. More than 1,400 people, both specialized staff and delegates, are currently on field missions for the [International Committee of the Red Cross] across the globe. This work is backed up by some 11,000 local employees and supported and coordinated by around 800 staff at its Geneva headquarters. (International Committee of the Red Cross, http://www.cicr.org)

Unit Assignment | Report on a global problem

In this section, you will deliver a group presentation on a global problem. As you prepare your presentation, think about the Unit Question, "What does it mean to be a global citizen?" and refer to the Self-Assessment checklist on page 50.

For alternative unit assignments, see the *Q: Skills for Success Teacher's Handbook*.

Consider the Ideas

In a group, discuss this campus flyer that introduces students to ways they can get involved in grassroots campaigns and become better global citizens on their own campus.

Informed Students ▸▸▸ **Global Citizens**

New students! Welcome to this month's edition of *Informed Students* ▸▸▸ **Global Citizens.**

You're in college now, and doors are open to the following organizations! Join up and make a difference.

Greenpeace: You've probably seen Greenpeace volunteers and recruiters around campus. They're here to encourage you to sign petitions to protect the whales and other endangered species. If you want to do more, why not sign up to be a volunteer yourself?

Habitat for Humanity: Although spring break is months away, check out a Habitat for Humanity working vacation to an area where hurricane victims get needed homes.

Humanities Out There: No need to go far from home to lend a hand. Underprivileged students nearby need tutors in English and math. Volunteer to help!

Campus Recyclers: Work at the recycling center collecting plastic bottles and paper and helping to raise awareness on campus about the need to recycle. Every little bit helps!

1. Discuss the issues these groups are involved in and the problems they are working to solve. What solutions do they offer?
2. Many grassroots organizations like these try to raise money, write letters to political leaders, or work on small projects that help people in need. What kind of work would you be willing to volunteer to do? How could an organization persuade others to volunteer?

Prepare and Speak

A. GATHER IDEAS **Work in a group. Think about the global problems and solutions discussed in this unit. Choose an issue related to the environment, health, education, energy, poverty, or a similar topic. Complete the chart with your group's ideas.**

What is the problem or issue?	
What are some of the causes of the problem?	
What are some of its effects?	
What are some possible solutions?	
What solutions or suggestions can your group offer?	

B. **ORGANIZE IDEAS** **Plan your group presentation.**

Tip for Success

To make sure points are not lost in a long discussion, signal importance by using introductory phrases and numbering points. *"Here's how it worked: First, they signed up volunteers. Second, they . . . "*

1. Divide the following parts of your presentation among your group members:
   a. Introduce and explain the problem
   b. Explain possible causes
   c. Discuss effects
   d. Present possible solutions
2. If possible, use information from outside sources in your presentation (you can research outside of class or use information from this unit).
3. Make note cards to remind you of what to cover during the presentation.
4. Practice your presentation. Time yourselves so that you keep to the limit set by your instructor. Give each other feedback on your sections of the presentation, and exchange suggestions for improvement.

C. **SPEAK** **Give your presentation to the class. Refer to the Self-Assessment checklist below before you begin.**

CHECK AND REFLECT

A. **CHECK** **Think about the Unit Assignment as you complete the Self-Assessment checklist.**

SELF-ASSESSMENT		
Yes	No	
☐	☐	I was able to speak fluently about the topic.
☐	☐	My group and class understood me.
☐	☐	I used vocabulary and collocations from the unit to express my ideas.
☐	☐	I used reported speech to cite information from others.
☐	☐	I linked final sounds to make my speech more fluent and understandable.
☐	☐	I cited sources appropriately and effectively.

B. **REFLECT** **Discuss these questions with a partner.**

What is something new you learned in this unit?

Look back at the Unit Question. Is your answer different now than when you started this unit? If yes, how is it different? Why?

Track Your Success

Circle the words and phrases you learned in this unit.

Nouns	Verbs	Adverb
accounting	afford 🔑	roughly 🔑
activist 🔑	devise	**Phrases**
commodity AWL	exploit AWL	accounting practices
co-op	guarantee 🔑 AWL	confidence of investors
economy 🔑 AWL	transform 🔑 AWL	core strategies
expenditure	**Adjectives**	emerging economy
intermediary	core 🔑 AWL	ethical goods
investor AWL	ethical AWL	household expenditures
processor	intangible	intangible assets
speculation	massive 🔑	labor standards
standard 🔑	proactive	social impact
	sustainable AWL	sustainable market

🔑 Oxford 3000™ words

AWL Academic Word List

Check (✓) the skills you learned. If you need more work on a skill, refer to the page(s) in parentheses.

LISTENING	○	I can organize notes with a T-chart. (p. 35)
VOCABULARY	○	I can use collocations. (p. 41)
GRAMMAR	○	I can use reported speech. (p. 43)
PRONUNCIATION	○	I can understand and use linking with final consonants. (p. 45)
SPEAKING	○	I can cite sources. (p. 47)
LEARNING OUTCOME	○	I can identify and report on aspects of a global problem.

UNIT 3

Size and Scale

LISTENING • listening for pros and cons
VOCABULARY • connotations
GRAMMAR • parallel structure
PRONUNCIATION • word stress patterns
SPEAKING • developing interview skills

LEARNING OUTCOME

Role-play interviews for a job or a school and be prepared to answer a question that is creative or unusual.

Unit QUESTION

Is bigger always better?

PREVIEW THE UNIT

A **Discuss these questions with your classmates.**

What can a large business offer its employees that a smaller company cannot? What can smaller businesses offer?

Do you prefer to have a large group of acquaintances or a small group of closer friends? Why?

Look at the photo. Do you prefer to shop in large stores or small stores? Why?

B **Discuss the Unit Question above with your classmates.**

Listen to Level 10(CM), Track 23 to hear other answers.

C Complete the survey. (If you are already in college or if you have finished college, think about how you would have answered in the past.)

Take a Quiz

cars · animals · school · science · tv · sports

RATE ★★★★★ | @ EMAIL | SHARE | Search [ ] Go

Small College or Large University—What's Best for You?

Answer the questions without thinking too long; just choose the answer that seems most attractive to you at first.

1. Do you know what you want to study?
   - A. Yes, I've known for years.
   - B. No, not yet. I want to see all the choices.
2. What kind of classes do you prefer?
   - A. Small classes with lots of lively discussion.
   - B. Lectures where I can listen and take notes.
3. What do you imagine doing on weekends?
   - A. Hanging out with a few good friends.
   - B. Anything social!
4. Do most of your friends know each other?
   - A. Yes. The same group has been together for a long time.
   - B. No, I have several different groups of friends, all very different from each other.
5. You hope your roommate in college will . . .
   - A. share a lot of the same interests.
   - B. be as different from you as possible!
6. Your college years are a time to . . .
   - A. concentrate on the skills and knowledge you'll need for your future career.
   - B. meet people and learn a lot of different things.

Now count your answers. Do you have more As or more Bs?

More *A* answers

You know what you want to study, and you have focused goals. A smaller college might work best for you. However, make sure that the one you choose has all of the courses that you want to take.

More *B* answers

You see this period of life as a time for exploring and trying new possibilities. A large university will offer you more variety. However, be careful not to spend all of your time experimenting! Your challenge will be learning to focus your energy.

Home | Join | Help | Contact Us | Privacy Policy | Terms of Use | Site Map   f Share 5

D Work with a group. Share and discuss your answers to the survey. Do you agree with your results? Why or why not? What are some other reasons students choose small colleges or large universities?

LISTENING

LISTENING 1 | Small Is the New Big

VOCABULARY

Here are some words and a phrase from Listening 1. Circle the correct word or phrase to complete each sentence. Use the context of the sentence to help you.

1. In some large cities, health problems can quickly become **widespread** because of the (close contact between / greater distances between) people.
2. In order to **facilitate** the admissions process and decrease the stress for new students, the university set up (easy online applications / difficult selective requirements).
3. During finals, even when **simultaneous** exams are being held across campus, students cannot take tests that are (too difficult to pass / given at the same time).
4. Because the **motto** of that organization is "The Customer Comes First," the workers try to live up to that (guiding belief / overall license) by providing good service.
5. When a company is **audited** due to suspicious activities, outside accountants are called in to (investigate / praise) its finances.
6. The company is **collapsing** due to negative changes in the industry; as a result, many workers have been (hired / fired).
7. The company does an exhaustive **feasibility** study before any investment is made in a new product. That means they do a study to see (if the product will succeed / if the product will be easy to use).
8. When two companies are said to be **in the same league**, they (play the same sport / have equal qualities or characteristics).
9. If interviewers ask you to rate your **flexibility**, they probably want to find out about your ability to (adapt to / teach about) changes in the workplace.
10. In order to save money, some companies **outsource** their work to (other organizations or countries / their own in-house employees).

motto: slogan, principle belief.

fired: kick out, let go dismissed, sacked

feasibility: usability

outsource: assign

11. If you (can / can't) find a job, you might go to an employment **agency**, which is an organization designed to match businesses with employees.

12. If you want to make an **investment** in your future, you should try to (limit money for / put your money into) education and job training.

Seth Godin

Preview Listening 1

Small Is the New Big

Seth Godin has an MBA from Stanford University and writes about business from his position as an entrepreneur—one who takes risks in starting businesses. You are going to listen to him read a chapter from his book *Small Is the New Big*.

What businesses, places, or things do you think Godin might say are better off being small? Check (✓) your guesses.

☐ an airline	☐ a computer	☐ a social networking site
☐ a bank	☐ a law firm	☐ a television
☐ a university	☐ a restaurant	☐ a city government

Why choose a big computer . . .

. . . versus a small computer?

Listen for Main Ideas

Level 10(CM)
Track 24

Listen to the audiobook chapter. Check (✓) the main ideas that represent Godin's point of view.

☐ 1. People used to trust big companies more.
☐ 2. Startup companies used to want to stay small so that they could be more efficient.

Chief organization officer

- [x] **3.** Organizations that once benefited from being big may now suffer from being too big.
- [x] **4.** One of the overall benefits of newer small operations is the personal contact between owners and the public.
- [ ] **5.** "Get Big Fast" is the motto for small companies today.
- [ ] **6.** Entrepreneurs have to learn to think small in order to make a small business successful.

LISTEN FOR DETAILS

Level 10(CM)
Track 25

Read the questions. Then listen again and write the answers.

1. What are three of the advantages of past big businesses that Godin mentions?

   power grow profit, control our supplies

2. Why does Godin feel that "big computers are silly"?

   use lot power, not efficient.

3. When listing smaller products that are better than big ones, what example does Godin give to illustrate the saying "An exception that proves the rule"?

   big screen tv

4. According to Godin, what does the example of free WiFi at the skateboard park demonstrate?

   because is easy and faster to do it

5. What can you infer from Godin's statement "Small means you can tell the truth on your blog"?

6. What kinds of jobs might a small company outsource and why?

manufacturing, shipping, boring stuff

7. What does Godin mean when he says, "A small venture fund doesn't have to fund big, bad ideas in order to put their capital to work"?

small investments in big ideas.

8. Godin asks, "Is it better to be the head of craigslist [the network of online communities, featuring free online ads] or the head of UPS [the worldwide package delivery service]?" How would he answer this question?

WHAT DO YOU THINK?

Discuss the questions in a group.

1. What does the expression "small is the new big" mean?
2. Do you agree with Godin that small businesses have a large advantage over big businesses today? Why or why not?
3. Which company would you rather work for, a smaller company like craigslist or a larger one like UPS? Why?

Listening Skill | Listening for pros and cons

Speakers can compare and contrast options by listing the **pros and cons**, or benefits and drawbacks. They may signal their intentions with phrases such as these.

There are some advantages and disadvantages . . .
Let's compare . . .
We'll examine both sides of . . .

When you can predict that a speech, lecture, or program will compare pros and cons, you can divide your paper into a T-chart and note information in the appropriate column.

Small restaurants

Pros	Cons
nice atmosphere	more expensive
owner greets you by name	less variety

Speakers often use transitions to show that they are going to present contrasting information. It is important to note the points being made about each of the sides discussed. Speakers may follow one of these patterns.

- Pros of A. Transition, cons of A.
- Pros of A. Transition, cons of B.
- Cons of A. Transition, pros of B.

Listen for organizational cues such as these:

on (the) one hand . . . on the other hand
on the other side
in contrast
but
however
yet
though

Listen to the organizational cues in these examples.

Level 10(CM)
Track 26

A large law firm may have many lawyers that specialize in different areas. **However**, smaller firms often hire lawyers who have better training.

On the one hand, craigslist probably has happier employees because it is small. **On the other hand**, it may lose employees who prefer to work for a bigger company.

Level 10(CM)
Track 27

A. **Listen to someone speak about the pros and cons of small-town and big-city life. Complete the chart. Use the organizational cues you hear to help you.**

Small town	
Pros	**Cons**
– knew everyone - cheaper	

Big city	
Pros	**Cons**
+ jobs, transport	- expensive - groceries in bus - play street

Level 10(CM)
Track 27

B. **Listen again. Write the organizational cues the speaker uses to signal pros and cons.**

1. in contrast to
2. however
3. on the one hand
4. on the other hand

LISTENING 2 | Sizing Up Colleges: One Size Does Not Fit All

VOCABULARY

Here are some words from Listening 2. Read the sentences. Circle the answer that best matches the meaning of each bold word or phrase.

1. "How Trade Influences Economics" is too broad a topic for your research paper; you'll need to **narrow** it to something more specific.
   a. expand   b. limit   c. double
2. **Countless** students have passed through the halls of this famous university since the college opened in 1821.
   a. numerous   b. uneducated   c. not enough
3. The terrible cold and pouring rain didn't seem to affect the **passion** of the sports fans at all; the stadium was packed full with cheering spectators.
   a. enthusiasm   b. understanding   c. hatred

4. The university liked to tell prospective students about the many **distinguished** graduates who had contributed to politics, business, and the arts.

   a. modest; shy   b. unpopular; controversial   c. successful; admired

5. The scientists finally received permission to **conduct** the sensitive and important experiment they needed to complete their research.

   a. perform   b. cancel   c. shorten

6. Traveling to a new city in a country where you don't speak the language can be **intimidating** until you get used to it and find your way around.

   a. inviting   b. scary   c. impossible

7. Many companies give **priority** to job applicants' work experience instead of their grades in college, which makes it difficult for new graduates to find work.

   a. moderate consideration   b. top importance   c. unfavorable attention

8. Do you think it's better for university students to concentrate on just one or two subjects or to study a **diversified** range of different subjects?

   a. specialized   b. simplified   c. varied

9. A careful **analysis** of the causes of the problem is necessary before anyone can propose a useful solution.

   a. study; examination   b. result; outcome   c. rejection; dismissal

10. More scholarships would **enable** students from low-income families to study at this expensive private school.

    a. prevent   b. inspire   c. allow

11. Before I book a room in a hotel, I like to check online to see if it has the **facilities** I enjoy, such as a good restaurant, a gym, and parking.

    a. rooms   b. abilities   c. features

12. In addition to looking at high school grades, college admissions officers look at applicants' participation in **extracurricular** activities such as sports and school clubs.

    a. academic   b. supplementary   c. required

PREVIEW LISTENING 2

Sizing Up Colleges: One Size Does Not Fit All

You are going to listen to a podcast about some pros and cons of attending big universities versus small colleges.

How common are the following features in small private colleges, large public universities, or both? Write the features into the Venn diagram. Discuss your ideas in a group before you listen to see if your ideas are correct.

- competitive sports teams
- large lectures
- medical schools
- dormitories
- personal advisers
- small classes
- high tuition
- teaching assistants
- social clubs

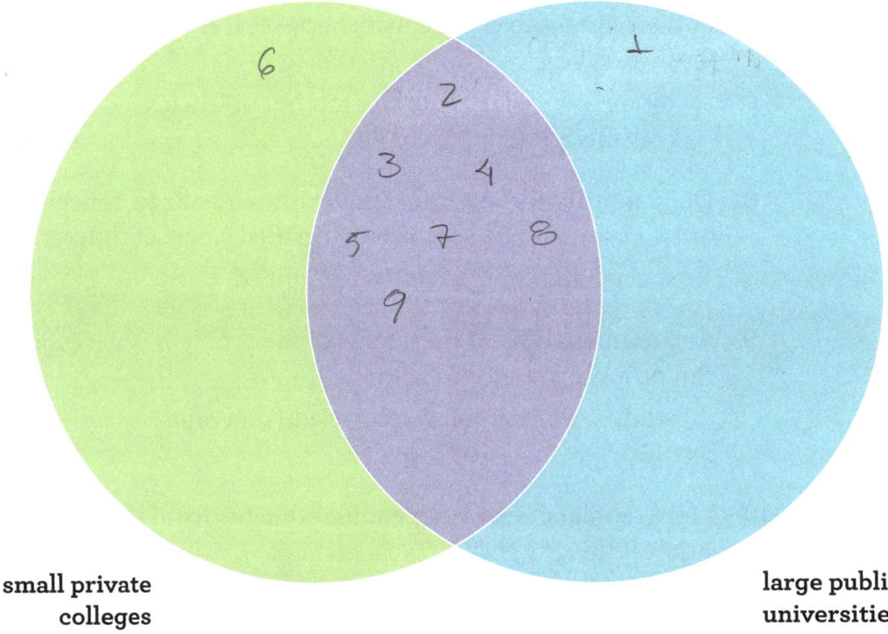

LISTEN FOR MAIN IDEAS

Level 10(CM)
Track 28

Read the questions. Then listen to the podcast. Write short answers.

1. What is the main purpose of this recording?

____

2. According to the first speaker, what should students think about when evaluating colleges?

____

3. What are the areas the speakers emphasize to highlight the differences between big universities and small colleges?

____

4. The subtitle of this podcast is "One Size Does Not Fit All." What do you think that means, and how do the speakers show this point?

____

LISTEN FOR DETAILS

Level 10(CM)
Track 29

A. Read the T-chart. Listen again to Part 1 of the podcast. Complete the chart.

Big schools: pros & cons

Pros	Cons
• more sports and other school activities	• courses taught by ________________, not professors
• endless options and countless ________________ programs	• professors focused on ________________ rather than teaching
• access to ________________ facilities	• more red tape and administrative procedures
• ability to work with graduate students	• introductory classes with ________________ of students
• ________________ professors	• problem of being unnoticed

Level 10(CM)
Track 29

B. Read the T-chart. Listen again to Part 2 of the podcast. Complete the chart.

Small schools: pros & cons

Pros	Cons
• hands-on learning opportunities __________ class sizes	• __________ research facilities
• classes taught by __________	• no __________ students to interact with
• opportunities to create your own major and curriculum and explore areas outside your field of study	• limited sporting events and other __________ activities
• strong sense of community	• difficulty moving in and out of social groups
• high level of __________ interaction	

What Do You Think?

A. **Discuss the questions in a group.**

1. What do you think is the most important advice the podcast gives to students deciding on a college?
2. How much thought did you put into choosing the school you are studying at now? What factors influenced your decision? At this point, do you think you made the right choice?

Tip Critical Thinking

In Activity B, you will **incorporate** information from different sources in your answers. Incorporating ideas from different sources is a way of synthesizing information.

B. **Think about both Listening 1 and Listening 2 as you discuss the questions.**

1. In what ways do the two Listenings help you answer the question "Is bigger always better?"
2. Do the two recordings give a balanced view of the pros and cons of big (and small) businesses or schools, or do the speakers present a biased view? Explain your reasons.

Vocabulary Skill Connotations

Words have **denotations**, or literal dictionary meanings, as well as **connotations**, which are the emotional or cultural associations the word evokes. We often characterize connotations as neutral, positive, or negative. For example, there are several words that refer to a person who weighs less than average. The word *thin* has a relatively neutral connotation, whereas *skinny* or *gaunt* are more negative, and *slender* is more positive. Understanding the connotation of words can help you understand and convey ideas more clearly.

A. Work with a partner. For each pair of words, indicate which word has the more positive (+) connotation and which has the more negative (–) connotation. Use a dictionary to check your ideas.

1. ___ passion ___ obsession
2. ___ economical ___ cheap
3. ___ fire (*v.*) ___ downsize
4. ___ assertive ___ pushy
5. ___ smile ___ smirk
6. ___ nerdy ___ studious
7. ___ notorious ___ distinguished
8. ___ gossip ___ talk
9. ___ lazy ___ relaxed
10. ___ persistence ___ stubbornness

B. Complete each sentence with one of the words from Activity A. With a partner, discuss the reasons some sentences sound more negative.

1. I think I need a new roommate—the one I have now is so _______________ that she won't even buy her own toothpaste.
2. One of Jim's best qualities is his _______________. He stays with a task until it is completed.
3. Two of my co-workers _______________ all the time, and I can't concentrate on my work.
4. I really like working in a(n) _______________ atmosphere. As long as everything gets done, I don't think the work environment needs to be stressful.
5. That actress is _______________ for her wild lifestyle. She's always in the news for some problem or another.
6. When I arrived, Tom kept looking at me with a funny _______________ on his face. I wondered what he was hiding.
7. I am so sorry to inform you that we have to _______________ staff. We just don't need all the employees we have now.
8. It's important to be _______________ when someone is intimidating you. You need to stand up for yourself.

SPEAKING

Grammar Parallel structure

When listing two or more things, it is important to maintain **parallel structure**. This means that your list should have the same pattern of words, phrases, or clauses. Parallel structure helps your listener understand that the ideas are connected and have the same level of importance. The words *or* and *and* usually come before the last item in a list.

Mixing words, phrases, and clauses will cause a break in the parallelism. If you read your sentences out loud, you can often hear that the rhythm has been broken when the items are not parallel.

✓ The small planes weren't in the same league as the larger ones that were **fast**, **efficient**, and **economical.** (parallel structure: adjectives)

✗ The small planes weren't in the same league as the larger ones that were fast, had efficiency, and economical. (non-parallel structure: mix of words and phrases)

✓ Students need to **attend class**, **complete assignments**, and **pass tests.** (parallel structure: verb + noun phrases)

✗ Students need to attend class, completion of assignments, and pass tests. (non-parallel structure: different types of phrases)

✓ I am a good candidate for the job because **I attended a good college**, **I have experience**, and **I am a hard worker**. (parallel structure: clauses)

✗ I am a good candidate because I attended a good college, my strong experience, and I am a hard worker. (non-parallel structure: mix of clauses and phrases)

Tip for Success

You can reduce clauses in a list to phrases by deleting a subject that is repeated in each: *He is distinguished because he is rich, owns a company, and has a good education.*

If you are listing three single items, remember that your voice pitch will rise at the end of the first two items and then fall at the end of the last one.

If you are listing three phrases, your voice pitch will rise on the last content word of each of the first two phrases and then fall at the end of the last content word in the final phrase. Notice the intonation of the following example:

Level 10(CM) Track 30

My adviser told me that I needed to **concentrate on my major**, (phrase)

find an internship, (phrase) and **do some research**. (phrase)

Level 10(CM)
Track 31

A. **Listen to the sentences and complete the chart by indicating whether the sentences are parallel or not parallel. Use intonation as a clue.**

	Parallel	Not parallel
1	☐	☐
2	☐	☐
3	☐	☐
4	☐	☐
5	☐	☐
6	☐	☐
7	☐	☐
8	☐	☐
9	☐	☐
10	☐	☐

B. **Work with a partner. Take turns using the prompts below to ask questions about businesses and schools. Include a list of at least three items in each answer.**

A: Can you give me three characteristics of a good company to work for?

B: A good company should pay employees well, have friendly bosses, and provide clean working conditions.

Ask about:

1. Three reasons you don't want to work for a big or small company
2. Three places you would like to work
3. Three reasons why you prefer a big city or a small town
4. Three reasons why you do or do not want to go to school in a different country
5. Three reasons that young children should go to a large or small school

Pronunciation | Word stress patterns

Words in English have different **stress patterns**. Using the correct pattern ensures that your listener will be able to understand what you are saying.

For example, many nouns in English fall into the 2-1 pattern: a two-syllable word with stress on the first syllable (*WIN-dow*, *COL-lege*, *OF-fice*). The first number represents the number of syllables. The second number indicates the number of the syllable that is stressed.

Remember that:

- stressed syllables have a longer beat and a higher pitch than unstressed syllables.
- unstressed vowels may be reduced to /ə/.
- suffixes often change the stress in a word.

Level 10(CM) Track 32

Listen to and repeat the examples.

2-syllable words	
2-1	**2-2**
founder	expand
passion	diverse
drawback	pursue

3-syllable words		
3-1	**3-2**	**3-3**
motivate	location	employee
agency	distinguish	volunteer
company	enable	reinforce

4-syllable words		
4-1	**4-2**	**4-3**
secretary	environment	academic
relatively	analysis	application
accurately	intimidate	independent

When learning a new vocabulary word, it is helpful to make a note of the syllable-stress pattern so you can make sure to pronounce it correctly.

Level 10(CM)
Track 33

A. Listen to the following words and circle the syllable you hear the speaker stress. Then label each word stress pattern (for example, as 2-1 or 4-3).

1. conducted ______
2. fortune ______
3. overwhelming ______
4. facilities ______
5. assistant ______
6. correct ______
7. corporation ______
8. socially ______
9. investment ______
10. audit ______
11. graduate ______
12. televised ______

Tip for Success

Organizing lists of academic words and terms in your field according to their stress patterns and reading the lists provide an efficient way to practice correct word stress and rhythm.

B. Work with a partner. Read the list of words you might use to describe yourself during an interview. Put each word in the correct column, based on the number of syllables and stress.

clever	efficient	independent	passionate
confident	energetic	intelligent	reliable
conscientious	experienced	mature	sociable
creative	gifted	motivated	talented
dependable	honest	organized	unique

2-1	2-2
	mature

3-1	3-2	3-3

4-1	4-2	4-3
motivated		

C. **Role-play an interview with a partner. Student A will choose some adjectives from the chart on page 70 and ask Student B if those adjectives describe him or her. Student B will respond and expand on one of the adjectives. Listen for correct word stress.**

A: Are you dependable and organized?

B: I am very dependable, but I'm not always organized when I'm under pressure.

Speaking Skill | Developing interview skills

Interviews can be stressful speaking situations. You can ease the stress by knowing what to expect and preparing for the questions. Practice responding to the interview questions in advance so that you will be relaxed and confident during the actual interview.

Before the interview:

- **Prepare:** Find out about the college or company so you know how to answer and ask questions.
- **Predict:** Develop a list of potential questions the interviewers might ask.
- **Practice:** Have a friend act as an interviewer and practice responding to the questions.

During the interview:

- Maintain good eye contact and don't be afraid to smile.
- Use a formal speaking style and avoid slang.
- Emphasize key words to show interest and enthusiasm.
- Avoid long pauses before responding. When necessary, ask for clarification.

Do you mean, would I be comfortable living in a dormitory?
Are you asking if I have taken any classes in statistics?
Since you are asking if I feel prepared to work in such a large organization, let me say that . . .

- Use expressions to fill in the gap while you are thinking of a response.

That's a good question.
Let me think about that for a minute.

- Leave on a positive note by thanking the interviewers and saying you look forward to hearing from them.

Level 10(CM)
Track 34

A. Listen to three interviews. Which person would you hire? What advice would you give the other candidates? Discuss the pros and cons of the candidates in a group.

B. Work in pairs. Choose a job or college interview situation and practice your interview skills. Use the questions in the chart and/or some of your own. Take turns being the interviewer and the applicant.

Questions for college applicants	Questions for job applicants
What about our college attracted you to apply here?	How did you hear about our company?
What do you know about our campus and student body?	What job experiences have you had that make you qualified for this job?
Do you have a passion for any particular career?	What do you expect to learn by working for us?
Why do you think this small/big college is right for you?	What special skills would you bring to the table?
What do you like most about your current school?	What is your long-term career goal?
Have you decided on a major yet, and if so, why did you choose it?	Do you think you would be happy working for such a large/small organization?
	Have you ever been fired from a previous position?

Unit Assignment | Role-play interviews for a job or a school

In this section, you are going to role-play interviews for a workplace or a school. As you prepare for your interview, think about the Unit Question, "Is bigger always better?" and refer to the Self-Assessment checklist on page 74.

For alternative unit assignments, see the *Q: Skills for Success Teacher's Handbook*.

CONSIDER THE IDEAS

A. Sometimes employers ask unexpected or unusual questions at an interview. Often there are no right or wrong answers; employers may be more interested in how candidates respond than what candidates say. They may be looking for creativity, clarity, confidence, and even a sense of humor. Read these examples of unusual interview questions and think about how you might respond to them.

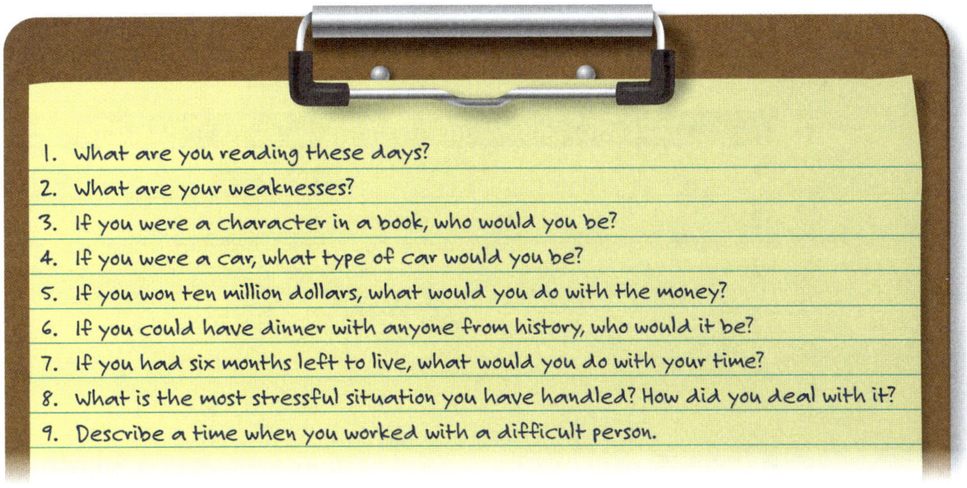

B. **What do you think an interviewer would hope to learn by asking these questions? How would you answer each one? Discuss your possible responses in a group.**

PREPARE AND SPEAK

A. **GATHER IDEAS** **Work in a group. Follow these steps to gather ideas.**

1. Decide if your group will conduct a business interview (with a committee of employers and staff interviewing candidates applying for a job) or an academic interview (with college admissions staff members interviewing applicants to the school).

2. Discuss the type of position or program that you are interviewing candidates for. What qualities would the ideal candidate have? List adjectives to describe the position or the candidate.

B. **ORGANIZE IDEAS** **Break into two smaller groups: interview committee members and candidates.**

Interview committee members: Choose five questions to ask each candidate. At least one should be creative or unusual. Write the questions below. Then divide the questions among the committee members.

1. ______________________________

2. ______________________________

3. ______________________________

4. ______________________________

5. ______________________________

Candidates: List five questions you predict the interviewers might ask you and note ideas for possible responses.

Possible questions	Possible responses
1.	
2.	
3.	
4.	
5.	

C. SPEAK Role-play your interviews. Refer to the Self-Assessment checklist below before you begin.

1. Interview committees: Write each candidate's name and ask the questions. Take notes on the pros and cons for each candidate. Interview candidates: Use your notes for possible questions and responses to help you answer the questions.
2. When the interviews are over, committees will briefly confer with each other, choose the best candidate, and tell the candidates who was selected and why.
3. As a group, discuss which questions were the most difficult to answer and which questions gave the most important information about the candidates.

Check and Reflect

A. CHECK Think about the Unit Assignment as you complete the Self-Assessment checklist.

SELF-ASSESSMENT		
Yes	No	
☐	☐	I was able to speak fluently in the interview.
☐	☐	My group understood me.
☐	☐	I used vocabulary with the appropriate connotations.
☐	☐	I used parallel structure when listing three or more ideas.
☐	☐	I stressed 2-, 3-, and 4-syllable words correctly.
☐	☐	I anticipated interview questions and practiced my answers to sound relaxed and natural.

B. **REFLECT** **Discuss these questions with a partner.**

What is something new you learned in this unit?

Look back at the Unit Question. Is your answer different now than when you started this unit? If yes, how is it different? Why?

Track Your Success

Circle the words and phrase you learned in this unit.

Nouns	Verbs	Adjectives
agency	audit	countless
analysis AWL	collapse AWL	distinguished
facilities AWL	conduct AWL	diversified AWL
feasibility	enable AWL	extracurricular
flexibility AWL	facilitate AWL	intimidating
investment AWL	narrow	simultaneous
motto	outsource	widespread AWL
passion		**Phrase**
priority AWL		in the same league

Oxford 3000™ words

AWL Academic Word List

Check (✓) the skills you learned. If you need more work on a skill, refer to the page(s) in parentheses.

LISTENING	I can listen for pros and cons. (p. 59)
VOCABULARY	I can use connotations. (p. 65)
GRAMMAR	I can use parallel structure. (p. 67)
PRONUNCIATION	I can speak with word stress patterns. (p. 69)
SPEAKING	I can develop interview skills. (p. 71)
LEARNING OUTCOME	I can role-play interviews for a job or a school and be prepared to answer a question that is creative or unusual.

UNIT 4

Alternative Thinking

LISTENING	distinguishing between facts and opinions
VOCABULARY	idioms and informal expressions
GRAMMAR	noun clauses
PRONUNCIATION	conditional modals: affirmative and negative
SPEAKING	using formal and informal language

LEARNING OUTCOME

Develop a marketing presentation designed to sell a new invention or idea.

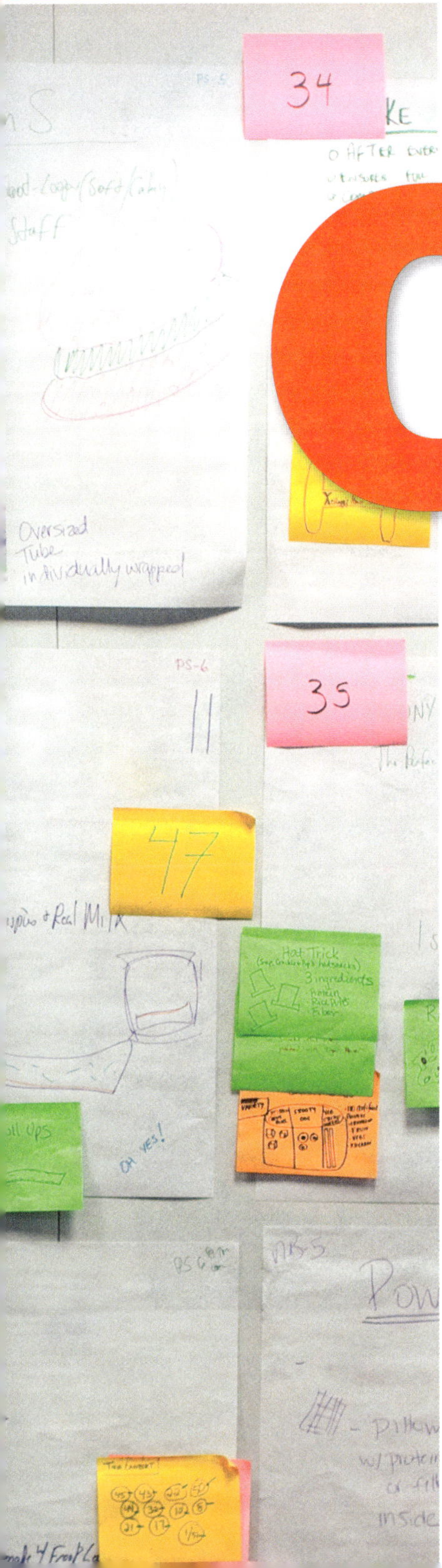

Unit QUESTION

Where do new ideas come from?

PREVIEW THE UNIT

A Discuss these questions with your classmates.

How do you come up with new ideas or solve problems? Where do you look for inspiration?

What do you think have been some of the best inventions in the past ten years?

Look at the photo. What do you think the two women are mapping out on the wall?

B Discuss the Unit Question above with your classmates.

Listen to Level 10(CM), Track 35 to hear other answers.

C **Complete the survey. Then share and explain your responses in a group. Give specific examples where you can. Discuss what your answers show about your personality.**

When you . . . , . . . what do you do?

1. want to decide what movie to see
   - ☐ read the newspaper or a magazine
   - ☐ talk to friends
   - ☐ read online reviews
2. are sick
   - ☐ use traditional or folk remedies
   - ☐ rely on mainstream medicine
   - ☐ try a new-age or alternative therapy
3. prepare a meal for friends
   - ☐ make a favorite family dish
   - ☐ try a new recipe from a magazine
   - ☐ check the refrigerator and use what's there
4. imagine where you'll live in the future
   - ☐ imagine a house like where you grew up
   - ☐ imagine a home like one you have visited or seen on TV
   - ☐ imagine a futuristic home
5. need a new cell phone
   - ☐ get a similar model to the one you have
   - ☐ carefully research new phones and their features
   - ☐ buy a popular model or one your friends recommend
6. fail at a task
   - ☐ give up on the task and do something else instead
   - ☐ ask someone for help
   - ☐ rethink your plan and start over
7. are faced with a problem
   - ☐ use a solution that worked in the past
   - ☐ think up a new solution
   - ☐ brainstorm several possible solutions

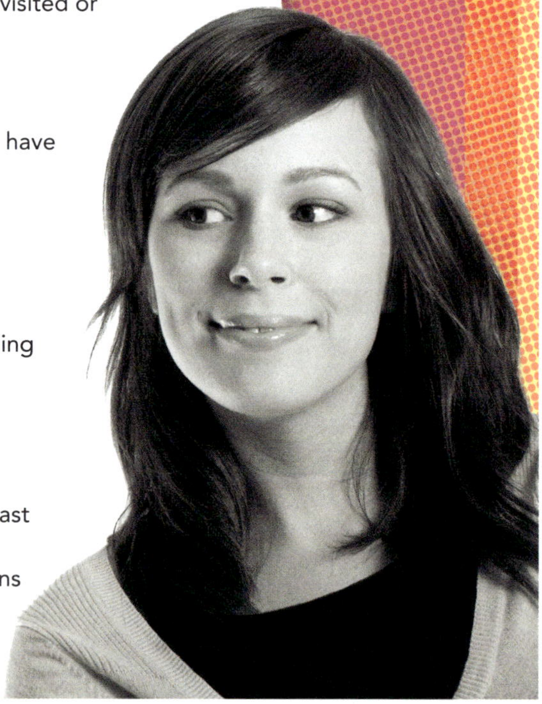

LISTENING 1 | Alternative Ideas in Medicine

VOCABULARY

Here are some words and phrases from Listening 1. Read the sentences. Cross out the word or phrase with a different meaning from the bold word or phrase.

1. Housing prices have increased because of the **shortage** of wood and other raw materials.
   a. poor quality b. scarcity c. lack
2. The appliances were packed in a large **container** for shipping.
   a. box b. carton c. house
3. Before you travel to France, you should **convert** your dollars to euros.
   a. change b. preserve c. transform
4. The space center built a **prototype** of the spacecraft to test it in a controlled environment.
   a. model b. diagram c. example
5. I'm **reluctant** to spend any more money on this failing project.
   a. hesitant b. excited c. unwilling
6. Please take a minute to **verify** the correct spelling of your name and address.
   a. confirm b. check c. hide
7. After adding two simple elements together, the scientist told us she had discovered a new **compound** that would cure a common cold.
   a. chemical reaction b. alternative medicine c. bonded mixture
8. You must follow the proper **protocol** for your experiment to be valid.
   a. procedure b. set of rules c. trend
9. My cousin applied for a visa, but unfortunately, he was **denied**.
   a. rejected b. refused c. reminded
10. I've heard **anecdotal evidence** that vitamin E helps cuts heal faster, but I've never read any research that supports that.
    a. scientific proof b. personal reports c. individual observations

11. It's important to review your investments **periodically**; my advisor recommends checking every three or four months.
    a. occasionally b. constantly c. regularly

12. All of his clever arguments still didn't **convince** me to change my mind.
    a. persuade b. prevent c. influence

Doc-in-a-Box, exterior

PREVIEW LISTENING 1

Alternative Ideas in Medicine

You are going to listen to two reports: "Doc-in-a-Box?" from WorldVision.org and "Bee Sting Therapy" from North Carolina Public Radio. They present innovative ideas that may benefit people's health.

With a partner, look at the photos. In the chart, list some typical uses of bees and of shipping containers. Then brainstorm some unconventional uses for them. Write down your ideas, and then share them with another pair.

Doc-in-a-Box, interior

a beekeeper

	Conventional uses	Unconventional uses
1. Bees		
2. Shipping containers		

LISTEN FOR MAIN IDEAS

Level 10(CM)
Track 36

A. Listen to the reports. Use the chart to take notes. Then compare notes with a partner and add any missing information.

	Report 1: Doc-in-a-Box	Report 2: Bee Sting Therapy
1. Meaning of the term and where it came from		
2. Problem it is trying to solve		
3. Analysis of the solution: Benefits		
4. Analysis of the solution: Obstacles		

Level 10(CM)
Track 36

B. Listen again. Then ask and answer the questions in pairs. Use your notes from Activity A to help you.

Report 1: Doc-in-a-Box?

1. What is the meaning of *Doc-in-a-Box*?
2. What problem is the Doc-in-a-Box program trying to solve? How is the program trying to solve it?

Report 2: Bee Sting Therapy

3. What is apitherapy and why does it work?
4. Why are the speakers so enthusiastic about this type of therapy?

Both Reports:

5. What are the main obstacles faced by those who try to present alternative ideas in medicine to the medical community?

LISTEN FOR DETAILS

Level 10(CM) Track 37

Read the statements. Then listen again. Write *T* (true) or *F* (false). Correct the false statements.

Report 1

____ 1. Laurie Garrett, founder of the Doc-in-a-Box idea, works for the Ministry of Health.

____ 2. Doc-in-a-Box medical centers could only offer medical care to poor people in cities near ports where ships could unload the containers.

____ 3. Ministries of Health or non-governmental agencies would operate the Doc-in-a-Box clinics.

____ 4. Garrett hopes that the Doc-in-a-Box clinics will mostly be staffed by doctors and paramedics from famous hospitals around the world.

____ 5. Garrett believes the container price could eventually go down from $5,000 to $1,500.

Report 2

____ 6. Frederique Keller is a nurse and an acupuncturist.

____ 7. It is difficult to travel with the bees.

____ 8. The idea behind apipuncture is to use the venom of dead bees to treat pain or discomfort.

____ 9. Andrew Cokin, a pain management doctor, says that the use of bee products already has a strong tradition in Asia and South America.

____ 10. According to former state legislator Fountain Odom, alternatives such as bee therapy are inexpensive and worth supporting.

WHAT DO YOU THINK?

Discuss the questions in a group.

1. In both of the reports in Listening 1, people have come up with a new use for something that has been around a long time. Can you think of any other inventions or therapies that are examples of the same principles?
2. Would you go to a doctor whose office was in a shipping container? Would you trust a bee to cure your pain? Why or why not?

3. In each of the two reports, do you feel that the narrator is taking a neutral position, or is he or she trying to persuade the listeners to accept or reject the idea? Explain your reasons.

Listening Skill Distinguishing between facts and opinions

A **fact** is something that is known to be true or that can be proven or disproven. An **opinion** is someone's personal belief. It cannot be proven or disproven. The ability to distinguish between facts and opinions helps you analyze the strength of a speaker's argument. It also helps you determine if the information provided is reliable. For example, we expect speakers to offer *support* for their opinions through their use of logic, examples, or facts.

Noticing certain words or phrases while you listen can help you identify whether a statement is a fact or an opinion.

Words or phrases identifying facts

- **Verbs that signal information or research:** *show, prove, verify, support, cause*
- **Numbers, statistics, or time periods to introduce facts:** *40 percent of, 15 students, for 200 years, since the early 20th century*
- **Expressions to introduce factual support:** *studies conducted, eyewitness reports, from the evidence, data reveal, studies have shown*

Words or phrases identifying opinions

- **Expressions to signal a belief, perception, or interpretation:** *I think, we believe, it seems, it appears*
- **Modals to signal advice, certainty, or possible solutions:** *should, must, could, might*
- **Adjectives that express judgments:** *best, worst, most important*
- **Adverbs and other words that show uncertainty:** *likely, probably, possibly, maybe, perhaps*

Level 10(CM) Track 38

Listen to these examples from Listening 1.

Facts: Bee venom has been used as a treatment since the time of the Greeks and for at least 2,000, 3,000 years in Chinese medicine.

Opinions: We believe that there are tremendous opportunities for the beekeepers of this state to develop some of the ancient modalities for medical treatment of pain and other uses. These are some alternatives that are very, very inexpensive.

Level 10(CM)
Track 39

A. **Listen to the sentences. Identify them as *F* (fact) or *O* (opinion). Write the word or phrase that helps you decide. Then compare answers with a partner. The first one is done for you.**

Sentence	Fact or Opinion?	Words / Phrases
1	*O*	*I think, unreliable*
2		
3		
4		
5		
6		
7		
8		
9		
10		

Level 10(CM)
Track 40

B. **Listen to this advertisement for an alternative medicine and complete the sentences with the words and phrases the speakers use. With a partner, talk about whether the ad relies mostly on fact or opinion to convince the audience. Then explain why you would or wouldn't buy the product.**

Go-Cream

Speaker: Have you noticed that your legs get tired in the middle of the day? Do you wish you could keep going when your body wants you to sit down? Do you have trouble keeping up with other people—or with life in general? Our ________ (1) product, Go-Cream, is the answer you've been looking for. It offers the ________ (2) solution for tired legs and low energy. After just one application of this energizing leg cream, you ________ (3) convinced. Made from the oils of the Brazil nut and sand from the beaches of Hawaii, Go-Cream soothes and energizes at the same time. ________ (4) of people suffer from tired legs, but now there is relief. Listen to what some of our satisfied customers have to say.

Customer 1: I'm a busy mother of four, and I've been using this product ________ (5). I've tried vitamins and other alternative therapies, but nothing worked—until Go-Cream. It's definitely ________________ (6) product out there and a deal at only $9.99 a jar.

Customer 2: ________________ (7) Go-Cream is for people of all ages. My friends and I are students, and we're always on the go. We've all tried Go-Cream and noticed a big difference in our energy. And it ________________ (8) even helps make your skin smoother and healthier, too.

Speaker: Don't get left behind. Order your Go-Cream today!

LISTENING 2 | Boulder Bike-to-School Program Goes International

VOCABULARY

Here are some words and a phrase from Listening 2. Read the sentences. Then write each bold word or phrase next to the correct definition.

1. I ride a bike to school occasionally, but my doctor says I really need to exercise **consistently** to improve my health.
2. When you have to give an **impromptu** speech, it's easy to make mistakes and forget to cover all the crucial information.
3. The **incentive** for trying out acupuncture is one month of free treatments.
4. Some supermarkets have automatic checkouts, where you scan the **bar codes** on your groceries yourself.
5. The organization made a **substantial** donation to our school, so we were able to buy 500 new computers.
6. The marketing department made some **outrageous** claims about the product that could not be proven.
7. What's the latest **buzzword** to get young adults excited about a new product?
8. A motor **propels** a car, but a bike is propelled by foot power.
9. Land in the countryside is cheaper to buy, but there is no existing **infrastructure**, such as water pipes and electric cables.

10. The committee **submitted** several plans to encourage children to participate in healthy activities.

11. The school district tried to get a **grant** to pay for bikes for children who couldn't afford one.

12. Before we can **implement** the new plan, we must get approval from management.

a. ______________________ *(n.)* a pattern of lines that contains information read by a computer

b. ______________________ *(n.)* the basic systems and services necessary for a country or city to run

c. ______________________ *(v.)* to give to somebody in authority for consideration; to hand in

d. ______________________ *(v.)* to move, drive, or push forward

e. ______________________ *(adj.)* large in value or importance

f. ______________________ *(adj.)* very unusual and slightly shocking

g. ______________________ *(v.)* to make something start to happen

h. ______________________ *(adv.)* repeatedly and in the same way

i. ______________________ *(n.)* a sum of money to be used for a specific purpose

j. ______________________ *(n.)* something that encourages somebody to do something; a reward

k. ______________________ *(adj.)* done without preparation or planning

l. ______________________ *(n.)* an expression or phrase that has become popular

Preview Listening 2

Boulder Bike-to-School Program Goes International

You are going to listen to a *Colorado Matters* radio interview with Tim Carlin, the executive director of a program called "Freiker." Carlin describes the idea he and his partner came up with to encourage children to ride bikes to school.

Check (✓) the ways you think kids could be encouraged to bike to school. Then listen to find out if any of them are mentioned as part of Carlin's plan.

- ☐ get praised by teachers and parents
- ☐ get an iPod
- ☐ get a water bottle
- ☐ get a certificate from the school
- ☐ get stickers
- ☐ get extra credit in a school class
- ☐ get healthy
- ☐ get a cash gift

Listen for Main Ideas

Level 10(CM)
Track 41

Listen to the interview. Write short answers. Then discuss them with a partner.

1. Where did the word "Freiker" come from, and why does the name of the program have to change?

   ____

   ____

2. How has the application of old and new technologies improved the way that the parents keep track of who is biking to school?

   ____

   ____

3. How does this program connect health, active transportation, and safety?

   ____

   ____

Listen for Details

Level 10(CM) Track 42

A. Listen again for the facts and complete the sentences with the correct information. Compare your answers with a partner.

1. The Freiker program at Crestview was started by two dads, and now about ________________ percent of the schoolchildren bike to that school.
2. The Freiker program has expanded to the states of Oregon and California in the U.S., and internationally to ________________.
3. The incentive offered to children who rode to school over 90 percent of the days was a(n) ________________.
4. The three main sources of funding for the Freiker program are ____.

B. Which of these two opinions might Carlin have? Discuss your choice with a partner.

1. It seems the incentives aren't working because fewer students are biking to school.
2. The Freiker program has been successful because technology has made it easier.

What Do You Think?

A. Discuss the questions in a group.

1. What are some advantages and disadvantages of offering children incentives to improve their health? What are some other ways to achieve the same goal?
2. Do you think it is possible to implement the Freiker program in every type of community? In what types of communities would it be easier? More difficult?

B. Think about both Listening 1 and Listening 2 as you discuss the questions.

1. Why is it challenging for some people to give up traditional methods for newer, innovative ones? What are some reasons others find it easy to make those changes?

2. Where should the money come from to support new ideas like the ones presented in this unit? How can people raise money or support for new ideas like these?

Vocabulary Skill | Idioms and informal expressions

Informal expressions can enrich your language when used correctly. However, informal language also affects the tone of the conversation or speech, and you should be very careful not to use informal language in the wrong situation. Here are some reasons people use informal language.

- To show that they belong to a certain group, such as young people or a certain club
- To show other people they are friendly, relaxed, or approachable
- To make a serious subject seem easier to understand

Most dictionaries indicate when words have an informal meaning (**kid** ▪ noun, *informal*) or are considered **slang** (**dude** ▪ noun, *slang*), meaning too informal and used only in conversation. Many **idioms** or set expressions are considered informal and are usually labeled (**IDM**) and listed in learners' dictionaries in a separate section at the end of an entry. Check the meaning of idioms and informal or slang expressions carefully before using them.

You can find an idiom by looking up the keyword—usually a noun or a verb—such as *think* in *think outside the box*. The keyword may not always be the first word in the expression. In addition, the idiom or informal expression may not always be the first meaning listed for a word. Look at these examples of idioms using the keyword *think*.

nothing of walking thirty miles a day. **think on your feet** to be able to think and react to things very quickly and effectively without any preparation **think outside (of) the box** to think about something, or how to do something, in a way that is new, different, or shows imagination **think straight** to think in a clear or logical way **think twice about sth/**

A. **Circle the keywords of these expressions. Then write a more formal expression for each one.**

Informal expression	More formal alternative
1. the buzz	news; rumors
2. just around the corner	
3. the deal is / here's the deal	
4. to catch on	
5. to get (something) off the ground	
6. a cut above (something)	
7. to wrap (something) up	
8. wild about (something)	

Level 10(CM) Track 43

B. **Listen to these excerpts from Listening 1 and Listening 2. Complete the sentences with the idiom or informal expression you hear. Discuss the meanings of each expression with a partner. Check a dictionary if necessary.**

1. **Rose Hoban:** But now Odom's a true believer. He says getting stung is the only thing that helps him with his pain. He's also convinced his wife, and that's ________________, since she's the state secretary for Health and Human Services.

   Meaning: ____________________________

2. **Rose Hoban:** Keller was here for the annual meeting of the American Apitherapy Society in Durham a couple of weeks ago. She demonstrated bee venom therapy during a session for about a dozen people who practically ________________ excitement as they waited to get stung.

   Meaning: ____________________________

Tip for Success

If you search the Internet for "business idioms," you will find many lists that include expressions such as *plug an idea*, *sell like hotcakes*, *cut a deal*, and *get off to a flying start*.

3. **Fountain Odom:** They might look at you askance or say, "Uh, you know, you are ________________, aren't you? I mean, why would you want to be stung by a bee?"

   Meaning: ________________________

4. **Laurie Garrett:** There was a description of a place called "Container City" in London in which shipping containers, painted in primary colors, had been stacked in unusual ways to create apartment buildings. And I, I simply thought of it at that moment and a little sort of "bingo" ________________ in my head.

   Meaning: ________________________

5. **Narrator:** Laurie Garrett, who now works with the Council on Foreign Relations, hopes governments and aid organizations will take her idea and ________________. She believes the container clinics, ultimately, could make portable medicine a reality for people in countries that need it most.

   Meaning: ________________________

6. **Tim Carlin:** So, once we felt that we had a really good day-to-day tracking system, we, um, well, Rob, the guy who, ah, really started the program, decided that, um, "Why don't we ________________ and offer a crazy incentive?" And, ah, his crazy incentive was an iPod.

   Meaning: ________________________

SPEAKING

Grammar Noun clauses

A **noun clause** is a group of words that functions as a noun. Like a noun, it can be a subject or a direct object in a sentence. It is a dependent clause and cannot stand alone as a sentence.

Noun clauses can combine two clauses, showing a connection between the ideas. To combine two statements, use *that*. Notice how the entire noun clause in the second sentence functions in the same way as the simpler noun in the first sentence.

The researchers explained the problem.
(The researchers = subject; explained = verb; the problem = direct object)

The government didn't support the protocol.
(The government = subject; didn't support = verb; the protocol = direct object)

The researchers explained **that** the government didn't support the protocol.
(main clause: The researchers explained — The researchers = subject; explained = verb)
(noun clause: that the government didn't support the protocol — the government = subject; didn't support = verb)

To combine a statement and a *Yes/No* question, use *if* or *whether*.

They don't know the answer. Can they verify the information in time?
They don't know **if they can verify the information in time.**

To combine a statement and a *wh-* question, use the *wh-* question word (*who, what, where, when, why*, or *how*).

I want to understand the issue. How do they change a container into a clinic?
I want to understand **how they change a container into a clinic.**

In a noun clause that begins with *if/whether* or a *wh-* question word, use sentence word order, not question word order.

✓ Scientists don't understand exactly why **bee sting therapy works.**
✗ Scientists don't understand exactly why does bee sting therapy work.

A noun clause can also be the subject of a verb, though this sounds very formal.

Where this program goes next is up to you to decide.
(Where this program goes next = subject)

A. Underline the noun clause in each sentence.

1. She believes the container clinics, ultimately, could make portable medicine a reality for people in countries that need it most.
2. I've had patients in the last 20 years who told me that relatives of theirs, older relatives working in the garden, had accidently got stung on their hands by a bee, and their arthritis got better.
3. And I might also add that we also include walkers now, um, as part of the program.
4. We see no reason why, if retrofitting is done on a mass scale . . . , these containers couldn't come in for well under $1,500 apiece.
5. Some compounds in bee venom might affect how the body transmits pain signals to the brain, but it's hard to know for sure.
6. He told me how this grew from a handful of kids at Crestview Elementary School in Boulder into an international program.

Tip for Success

It is common to delete the word *that* before noun clauses in speaking, but not in writing. *Garrett says [that] the cost of the clinics could be less.*

B. Work with a partner. Take turns reading the sets of two short sentences and combining them by using a noun clause.

A: Should I invest in that new product? I'm not sure.

B: I'm not sure if I should invest in that new product.

1. He thought that his coworker had stolen his idea. He told his boss.
2. Do we want to sell it online? We aren't sure.
3. Where did they develop the prototype? I need to find out.
4. How did they raise enough money to give away iPods? It's not clear.
5. Why can't we convince people to get stung by bees? I don't understand.
6. Can they convince the public to buy it? They are trying to decide.
7. When was the product featured on the air? We are trying to find out.
8. The incentive could be seen as too outrageous. The group was worried.

Pronunciation Conditional modals: affirmative and negative

The auxiliary verbs *have* and *has* in conditional modal expressions such as *could have*, *would have*, and *should have* have a weakened **reduced form** when spoken. You may hear only the /v/ sound or what sounds like the word *of*.

In addition, in the negative contracted forms *couldn't have*, *wouldn't have*, and *shouldn't have*, the /t/ sound is not said distinctly. Therefore, it can be difficult to know whether you have heard *could have* or *couldn't have*!

To tell the difference, listen for the number of syllables (beats). *Could have*, even when the *have* is reduced, has two syllables. *Couldn't have* has three syllables.

Level 10(CM) Track 44

Listen and repeat these sentences.

I could have told her.
I couldn't have told her.
You should have come on Sunday.
You shouldn't have come on Sunday.
We would have been happy with that answer.
We wouldn't have been happy with that answer.

Level 10(CM) Track 45

A. Listen to the sentences. For each, circle *A* (affirmative) or *N* (negative).

1.	A	N	5.	A	N
2.	A	N	6.	A	N
3.	A	N	7.	A	N
4.	A	N	8.	A	N

Level 10(CM) Track 46

B. Practice the conversations with a partner. Pay attention to the modal expressions. Then listen to check your pronunciation.

1. **A:** Did you read about that woman who tried bee sting therapy? That's crazy! I wouldn't have done something like that. Would you?

   B: Well, I'm not sure. I would have researched it first, of course. I wouldn't have dismissed it without finding out about it, though.

   A: I wonder if it helped her at all. Perhaps she should have gone to a conventional doctor.

   B: But the article said that her arthritis was completely cured. Maybe you should have finished reading it.

2. **A:** I went to an amazing conference on alternative medicine yesterday. You should have been there. You would have loved it.

B: I know, but I had a big test to study for. If I hadn't studied, I wouldn't have passed. What did I miss?

A: Well, the best part was this guy who talked about using shark fin extract to help boost your immune system. I wouldn't have imagined that was possible. But he convinced me and even gave out some free samples.

B: Really? Maybe if I had been there, I could have tried one of those shark fin samples. I think I'm getting a cold.

Speaking Skill — Using formal and informal language

Deciding when to use formal and informal language, or appropriate **register**, is an important speaking skill. Register is reflected in the words, expressions, and pronunciation that speakers use.

Different situations and different audiences determine the register you should use. For example, it is too informal to use words like *stuff* and *awesome* when giving an academic presentation. However, it is too formal to try to convince a friend to look at your new cell phone by saying, "I would like you to examine this phone." You would probably just say, "Hey, check this out!"

In general, English speakers use more formal language with people they don't know or people of a higher social status and more informal language with friends or family members. However, the situation itself is also important. You might use informal language with an older, unfamiliar person in a relaxed social situation such as a party or a picnic. You might use more formal language if you were asking a close friend for a large favor or delivering some difficult or bad news.

Formal register uses . . .	Informal register uses . . .
uncontracted forms such as *cannot, did not, he would*	more contractions such as *can't, didn't, he'd*
discourse markers such as *I see, Yes, Actually, Exactly*	discourse markers such as *OK, Yeah, Sure, Well, Oh*
more passive voice	more active voice
standard English vocabulary	idioms, informal expressions, and slang
more one-word verbs	more phrasal verbs
longer, more complex sentences	shorter sentences

A. **In what ways would your use of formal or informal language differ in these three situations? Discuss your points with a partner.**

1. Explaining to your friend how you damaged his car in an accident / Reporting an accident in your friend's car to your insurance company
2. Explaining to your sister or brother why you had to buy the latest technology gadget / Explaining to your parents why you needed a new technology device
3. Telling your friend about a new social networking site you found. / Giving a report to your class about a social networking site

B. **Work with a partner. Choose one of the situations in Activity A or a similar one. Write a conversation. Make sure you use appropriately formal or informal language. Practice your conversation, and then present it to another pair or the class.**

Unit Assignment | Market a new idea

In this section, you are going to prepare a short presentation to "sell" a new invention or idea. As you prepare your presentation, think about the Unit Question, "Where do new ideas come from?" and refer to the Self-Assessment checklist on page 98.

For alternative unit assignments, see the *Q: Skills for Success Teacher's Handbook*.

CONSIDER THE IDEAS

Level 10(CM)
Track 47

A. **Listen to these two marketing presentations for a new product, the Vibrating Wallet. One presentation is for an audience of businesspeople looking to invest in a new product. The other is for an audience of young adult consumers. Take notes on types of language the speakers use in each ad. Listen for formal and informal expressions, facts and opinions, and reduced forms. Compare notes with a partner.**

B. Discuss these questions in a group.

1. What problem is this invention trying to solve?
2. Does this product recycle old ideas, demonstrate alternative thinking, or combine old and new ideas?
3. How does each marketing presentation attempt to appeal to the two different audiences? Are the presentations effective? What other suggestions might you offer to help sell this product to these audiences?
4. Would you buy this product? Why or why not?

PREPARE AND SPEAK

Tip Critical Thinking

In this Unit Assignment, you will discuss possible inventions that can solve a problem. When you **invent** solutions, even in your imagination, you are applying knowledge to create something new.

A. GATHER IDEAS Work with a partner. Discuss possible inventions or solutions to these problems or one of your own. Be creative.

Problem	Invention / Solution
1. remembering to take back your credit card	
2. losing your cell phone or mp3 player	
3. forgetting all of your Internet passwords	
4. not having enough time to clean your house	
5. spending too much money for public transportation	
6. (your own idea) ______________________	

B. ORGANIZE IDEAS Follow these steps to organize your ideas.

1. Work with your partner. Choose one problem and invention or solution from Activity A. You will make a presentation to a large group of business investors or a small gathering of young customers. Decide whether your presentation will be formal or informal.

2. Write an outline with notes for your presentation. Use this format.

    I. Introduction
    II. Problem / existing situation
    III. Description of invention / solution
    IV. Benefits or advantages of invention / solution
    V. Conclusion

3. Write note cards with your key ideas and any special language you want to use. Divide the presentation material so that each partner speaks for about the same amount of time.

C. **SPEAK** **Practice your presentation a few times. Then give it to a group or the whole class. Refer to the Self-Assessment checklist below before you begin.**

CHECK AND REFLECT

A. **CHECK** **Think about the Unit Assignment as you complete the Self-Assessment checklist.**

SELF-ASSESSMENT		
Yes	No	
☐	☐	I was able to speak fluently about the topic.
☐	☐	My partner and my group or class understood me.
☐	☐	I used noun clauses correctly.
☐	☐	I used vocabulary to talk about innovations, problems, and solutions.
☐	☐	I pronounced affirmative and negative conditional modals correctly.
☐	☐	I distinguished between facts and opinions and used them appropriately.
☐	☐	I used formal and informal language correctly.

B. **REFLECT** **Discuss these questions with a partner.**

What is something new you learned in this unit?

Look back at the Unit Question. Is your answer different now than when you started this unit? If yes, how is it different? Why?

Track Your Success

Circle the words and phrases you learned in this unit.

Nouns
bar code
buzzword
compound
container 🔑
grant 🔑 AWL
idiom
incentive AWL
infrastructure AWL
protocol AWL
prototype

Verbs
convert 🔑 AWL
convince 🔑 AWL
deny 🔑 AWL
implement AWL
propel
submit AWL
verify

Adjectives
impromptu
outrageous
reluctant AWL
substantial 🔑

Adverbs
consistently AWL
periodically AWL

Phrases
anecdotal evidence
shortage of

🔑 Oxford 3000™ words
AWL Academic Word List

Check (✓) the skills you learned. If you need more work on a skill, refer to the page(s) in parentheses.

LISTENING	○ I can distinguish between facts and opinions. (p. 83)
VOCABULARY	○ I can use idioms and informal expressions. (p. 89)
GRAMMAR	○ I can use noun clauses. (p. 92)
PRONUNCIATION	○ I can pronounce reduced forms. (p. 94)
SPEAKING	○ I can use formal and informal language appropriately. (p. 95)
LEARNING OUTCOME	○ I can develop a marketing presentation designed to sell a new invention or idea.

OXFORD
UNIVERSITY PRESS

Oxford University Press is a department of the University of Oxford. It furthers the University's objective of excellence in research, scholarship, and education by publishing worldwide. Oxford is a registered trade mark of Oxford University Press in the UK and in certain other countries.

Published in Canada by
Oxford University Press
8 Sampson Mews, Suite 204,
Don Mills, Ontario M3C 0H5 Canada

www.oupcanada.com

First Edition published in 2014
ISBN: 978-0-19-901354-8 ILSC English Communication 10: Q Skills for Success

Previously published as part of:
Q Skills for Success Listening and Speaking 5 Student's Book
© Oxford University Press 2011

Q: Skills for Success was originally published in English in 2011.
This edition is published by arrangement with Oxford University Press, Great Clarendon Street, Oxford 0X2 6DP, United Kingdom.

Oxford University Press is committed to our environment.
Wherever possible, our books are printed on paper which comes from responsible sources.

Printed and bound in the United States of America

1 2 3 4 — 17 16 15 14

ACKNOWLEDGEMENTS

The Publisher would like to thank the following for their kind permission to reproduce photographs: Back cover: ILSC Education Group; p. 2 Angelo Cavalli/Getty Images; p. 4 Image Source/Corbis; p. 6 Wolfgang Kaehler/SuperStock; p. 12 Bob Devan/Masterfile; p. 28 © Caro/Alamy; p. 30 (l–r) © James Boardman/Alamy; JOHN SHAW/SCIENCE PHOTO LIBRARY; Robert Harding Picture Library/SuperStock; p. 32 © Ariel Skelley/Corbis; p. 34 Photodisc/Oxford University Press; p. 36 © Thierry BrŽsillon/GODONG/Godong/Corbis; p. 38 © Image Source/Corbis; p. 52 © B.O'Kane/Alamy; p. 56 (l–r)Andrew Harrer/Bloomberg via Getty Images; Brian Finke/Getty Images; © KIMBERLY WHITE/Reuters/Corbis; p. 58 (l) Image Source/Oxford University Press; (r) © Matthias Ritzmann/Corbis; p. 62 (t) Getty Images; (bl) © Peter Titmuss/Alamy; (br) G Fiume/Getty Images; p. 71 © Holger Scheibe/Corbis; p. 76 Chris Strong/Getty Images; p. 78 (t) © -Mosquito-/iStockphoto; (b) © antsmarching/iStockphoto; p. 80 (l–r) Council on Foreign Relations/Ken Levinson; Council on Foreign Relations/Ken Levinson; © Vladimir Godnik/moodboard/Corbis; p. 84 Razumovskaya Marina Nikolaevna/Shutterstock; p. 87 © StockShot/Alamy

Illustrations by: p. 25 Stacy Merlin; p. 49 Stacy Merlin; p. 54 Karen Minot; p. 78 Stacy Merlin; p. 96 Marc Kolle